Against the Left

Thanks so much to the LRC readers who
helped sponsor this book, and special
gratitude to these generous benefactors:

Anonymous
Gary and Nina Turpanjian

~

Anonymous; Angelo Kelly; James Kluttz

~

Steven R. Berger

~

Bill Haynes, CMI Gold and Silver Inc.
Death to Tyrants Podcast
Jim Dernbach; Dan Glovak; Charles C. Groff
Richard Gullotti; Roxy Lewis; WhyNotGOLD
Tom McGinn, M.D.; Mark McKibben
Elijah Minton; Ernest L. Ortiz; William H. Sexton
Dirck Storm; Anne Williamson

Against the Left

A Rothbardian Libertarianism

LLEWELLYN H. ROCKWELL, JR.

LEWROCKWELL.COM

The daily news and opinion site LewRockwell.com was founded in 1999 by anarcho-capitalists Lew Rockwell and Burt Blumert to help carry on the anti-war, anti-state, pro-market work of Murray N. Rothbard.

Lew Rockwell.com
P.O. Box 1189
Auburn, Alabama 36831-1189
lewrockwell.com

ISBN: 978-0-9904631-5-3 (paperback)

The greatest obstacle to the spread of the philosophy of freedom described in Against the State *is the ideology of the left. The Left wants to destroy the traditional institutions of civil society, especially the family. It wants to wipe out all differences between people and make us "equal" slaves of the all-powerful State.*

Contents

Preface

by Hans-Hermann Hoppe

EVERY PERSON, INCLUDING IDENTICAL twins, is *unique*, different from and unequal to all other persons. Everyone is born at a different time and/or place. Everyone has two different, older and unequal biological parents, a male father and a female mother. Every person, throughout its entire life, faces and must act in a different and unequal environment with different and unequal opportunities and challenges, and every person's life, its accomplishments and its failings, its joys and satisfactions as much as its disappointments, sorrows and sufferings, then, is different from and unequal to that of everyone else. Moreover, this natural inequality of any and all human beings is still greatly amplified with the establishment of any and every society based on the division of labor.

The Left and socialism generally has always felt offended, enraged and scandalized by this natural inequality of man and has propagated and promoted instead a program of "equalization" or "egalitarianism," i.e., of "correctively" reducing, minimizing and ultimately eliminating all human differences and inequalities. Aptly, Murray Rothbard has identified this program as "a revolt against nature." This verdict notwithstanding, however, support for egalitarian ideas and promoters has never been in short supply as there are everywhere and always will be plenty of people clamoring that they have come up short in life as compared to others.

Hence, in order to advance their egalitarian utopia (or rather dystopia), every human characteristic, condition and institution smacking of difference and inequality, then, has been taken under attack by the Left in due course. Down with human excellence and all ranks of human achievement, because no person is to be more excellent than any other. Down with private property as it implies the distinction between mine and thine and thus renders everyone unequal. Down with all income differences. Down with the family as citadel of inequality, with a male father and a female mother and their common, young and dependent children. Down in particular with men and especially white men as the most unequal people of all. Down with marriage because of its exclusivity, and down with heterosexuality. Down with discrimination and individual preferences of and for one person over another. Down with free association and disassociation. Down with all covenants, and down with any and all borders, fortifications or walls separating one person from another. Down with exclusive, bi- or multi-lateral private contracts. Down with employers and landlords as unequal and different from employees and renters, and down with the division of labor in general. Down with the biblical notion that man is to rule and be the master of nature and rank above all animals and plants — and always down with everyone dissenting from the egalitarian leftist creed.

In *Against the Left*, Lew Rockwell, outstanding student of economist-philosophers Ludwig von Mises and Murray Rothbard, prolific author and, with the establishment of the Ludwig von Mises Institute, in Auburn, Alabama, foremost promoter and intellectual entrepreneur in the contemporary world of all matters and ideas "libertarian," i.e., of private property rights and human freedom, presents a detailed and vivid account of the leftist revolt against nature. He describes and analyzes the successive advances and growing influence of leftist ideas, in particular in the US but more generally also in the entire so-called Western world, and he explains and lays bare the disastrous or even horrifying effects, both morally and economically, that the steady leftist "progress" has had on the social fabric. Above all, as Rockwell explains, the price to be paid for the relentless revolt against human nature, for the stubborn pursuit of a goal that plainly cannot be achieved, is the rise and growth of an increasingly totalitarian State, controlled and run on a permanent basis by some small, exclusive elite of ruling "equalizers" standing above, separate and unequal from everyone else as their subjects and to-be-equalized human "material."

Rather than repeating what is stated and explained with utmost clarity by Rockwell in the following pages, I shall add only a few historical observations that may be helpful to the reader in gaining a better background understanding of the present age, brilliantly described then by Rockwell. They are observations from a European and still more specifically German perspective, the very countries where modern socialism first sprung up in the course of the 19th century and that have since had the longest experience with it, and they concern the different strategies and strategic changes that the Left has adopted to reach its present "high."

The "orthodox" strategy for socialist transformation, advocated by Marx and the followers of his so-called "scientific" socialism, was a revolutionary one. The Industrial Revolution in England and Western Europe had brought about a steadily growing number of industrial workers, i.e., of "proletarians," and this growing mass of proletarians, then, united by a common class-consciousness, was to expropriate all private owners of the means of production, i.e., the capitalists, in one fell swoop so as to supposedly make everyone an equal co-owner of everything. This would require a "dictatorship of the proletariat" as a temporary measure, but this transitory phase then would soon give way to a classless society and a life of equal plenty and happiness.

The orthodox strategy of socialist transformation turned out to be an utter failure. In the industrialized or industrializing countries of Western Europe, the growing proletarian masses showed little if any revolutionary fervor. They apparently felt that they had more to lose from the violent overthrow of the *ancien régime* and its old elites than only their chains. Instead, contra Marx, the revolutionary approach succeeded only in predominantly rural and agricultural Russia, with lots of peasants but no industrial proletariat to speak of. There, in the aftermath of a lost war, with the help of a strategic lie, i.e., the quickly broken socialist promise of liberating the Russian peasants from all feudal bonds and distributing all feudal landholdings as private property among the peasantry, and by means of massive and ruthless violence, of murder and mayhem, the czar and the old ruling elites were overthrown and a dictatorship of the proletariat established. But this dictatorship did not then give way to a classless society of equal plenty. To the contrary, as Mises had predicted from the outset, it resulted in the loss of all human freedom and in economic disaster. Without private property in land and other factors of production, everyone was rendered directly and immediately subject to the commands of the proletarian dictators; and these dictators, then, without private ownership of capital goods and hence without capital goods prices, were rendered incapable of economic calculation, with the inescapable result of permanent resource misallocation, economic waste and capital consumption. After about 70 years, the socialist "experiment" in Soviet-Russia imploded in a most spectacular fashion under its own weight, leaving behind an economic wasteland and a demoralized, deracinated, and impoverished population

The alternative, "revisionist" strategy of socialist transformation, largely adopted in the countries of Western Europe, was a reformist or gradualist one. With the steadily growing number of proletarians, it was only necessary under the given conditions to promote the already popular egalitarian idea of democracy and agitate for the systematic expansion of the franchise. Then, with the spread of democracy, a "peaceful" socialist takeover would become only a matter of time. And indeed, with the "right to vote" increasingly distributed "equally," to ultimately everyone, egalitarian motives and desires everywhere were systematically encouraged and strengthened all-around. The popularity of explicitly socialist parties steadily rose and all other, rival parties or ideological movements, including also the classical liberals, drifted increasingly leftward as well. At the end of World War I, then, with the legitimacy of the old regime and its ruling elites severely damaged by the devastations brought on by the war, the socialists appeared on the verge of victory. They failed, however, because of a fundamental misjudgment that had already become apparent with the onset of the Great War.

The revisionist socialists, not different from their orthodox comrades in this regard, were "internationalists." Their slogan was "proletarians of all countries unite." They believed in the solidarity of all workers, everywhere, against their common capitalist enemy. The war was proof that no such international worker solidarity existed. German workers willingly fought against workers from France, England, Russia, etc., and vice versa. That is, national attachments and national solidarity proved to be much stronger than any class attachment.

For this very reason also, and against the often violent resistance of the (internationalist) socialists, then, it would not be they who came to power, but rather explicitly nationalist socialist parties. All across Western Europe egalitarian sentiments were rampant. But the egalitarianism generally only went so far. It stopped when it came to foreigners, the people of other nations, especially when they were perceived as less wealthy than one's own. In addition, the triumph of nationalist socialism over international socialism in most of Western Europe and for the entire interwar period, was further assisted by the increasing spread of news from Soviet-Russia. The socialists in the West generally looked with great sympathy upon the "great experiment" conducted by their comrades in the East, and as Soviet sympathizers, then, their popularity profoundly suffered, the more information spread to the West about the ruthless cruelty of the Soviet dictators and social-ist Russia's desperate economic conditions, with wide-spread hunger and starvation. Moreover, not least in light of the Soviet experience, the nationalist socialists did not aim to expropriate all capitalists and national-ize all factors of production. Rather, more "moderately," they would leave all private property nominally intact and make sure "only" that it would be employed as the ruling nationalist socialist dictators saw fit, according to their motto that the "common good" always trumps any "private good."

With the outcome of World War II, the world dra-matically changed and socialists of all stripes found themselves confronted with new and radically differ-ent challenges. The US emerged from the war as the world's dominant superpower and Western Europe was essentially turned into a vast region of vassal states. Most importantly, (West) Germany as the principal European enemy country was placed under direct US control.

Nationalist socialist sentiments in Western Europe did not disappear on account of this development — and they remain popular to this day. Indeed, national socialist tendencies in the meantime had also taken hold in the US. The economic agenda and so-called social policies implemented by Roosevelt with the New Deal were essentially the same as those also pursued by Mussolini and Hitler. But the label nationalist socialist had to go down in infamy. By no means had all nation-alist socialist movements or parties during the inter-war period in Western Europe been tinged with racism or imperialism. But the especially odious example of defeated national socialist Germany had forever tarred the name, and all national socialist or fascist movements henceforth had to sail under different labels. Whatever their new names, however, their program now would typically entail also a good dose of anti-Americanism.

Other challenges arose for the internationalist or "left" socialists. With the onset of the Cold War between the US and its erstwhile Soviet allies who had expanded its control over most of Central Europe as a result of the war, the Left in US dominated Western Europe came under increasing pressure to distance itself from its comrades in the East. As well, similarly disastrous economic consequences in the Soviet dominated countries of Central Europe as those experienced in Russia before compelled the left socialists to successively abandon their original goal of the socialization of all means of production. As their nationalist socialist arch-enemies before, they would not eliminate private property and the private ownership of capital goods. Instead, they would allow for "as much private property and market as possible," but assure at the same time "as much State as necessary," with the decision as to what was "possible" and what was "necessary" made by the leadership of the socialist parties (just as the decision about how much "private good" and how much "common good" to have had been made previously by the national socialist leadership). As representatives of the industrial working class, the socialists would then use this decision-making power to equalize first "incomes" and then "opportunity" by means of taxation and legislation. And they would determine how much taxation and legislation was required to reach or approach this goal.

With this program the Left would ride to power in many countries across Western Europe. To achieve this success and in particular to maintain it, however, another strategic turn was required. In the course of European economic development, the number of industrial workers, i.e., the traditional "blue collar" working class, that made up the great bulk of the socialist voter base gradually but steadily declined. In order to stabilize and expand their voter base, socialists would have to shed their public image as the "party of proletarians" and appeal also to the steadily growing class of "white collar" workers and of service-industry employees. With the power to tax and redistribute private property and income, they would have to systematically increase the number of tax-funded "public sector" workers, i.e. of State-dependents, and in particular of workers in the so-called "social services" industry. Most importantly, in order to acquire an aura of intellectual respectability and authority, socialists would have to expand, infiltrate and ultimately takeover the entire system of "public education," from the universities on down to elementary schools and even kindergartens. The strategy worked. In particular, all across Western Europe universities and schools were brought under control of the egalitarian Left, and their increasing dominance of all of public debate, then, brought about a systematic leftward shift throughout the entire spectrum of political parties and movements.

Last but not least, new and different challenges for the socialists arose in the area of foreign affairs. As an internationalist movement, the Left aimed at establishing socialism everywhere, ultimately throughout the entire world, and they were supportive of attempts at political centralization as a means for the goal of supranational equalization. But they were also anti-colonialists, anti-imperialists and anti-militarists. Every country was supposed to liberate itself from its own foreign or domestic oppressors in order to then join in the international brotherhood of man on its own account.

When, already shortly after the war, the process of "European Integration" was launched, that would eventually lead to the "European Union" (in fact, a membership cartel of national State governments, with Germany as the economically strongest but political weakest member), the Left showed itself overwhelmingly supportive. The process was defective in that it started and proceeded under the tutelage of the US, but it also offered the opportunity of expanding egalitarian socialist power ultimately all across Europe. Less enthusiasm, and indeed considerable opposition from the Left encountered another US project: the establishment of NATO. As an international military alliance under supreme command of the US, many perceived and opposed NATO as a militaristic enterprise. But in light of the "Soviet Threat," i.e., the systematically popularized and over-dramatized danger of a military takeover of Western Europe by the Soviet Union, any serious opposition would be quickly silenced and NATO membership was embraced by the Western European Left as well.

With the collapse of the Soviet Union and its Empire in the early 1990s, a similar challenge again arose for the socialists. With the disappearance of the Soviet threat and the end of the Cold War, NATO had accomplished its goal and apparently no longer fulfilled a purpose. Yet NATO was not dissolved as most (but not all) of the Left wished it would. To the contrary.

After some momentous victories of the egalitarian Left in the US since the 1960s, with the so-called Civil Rights movement and legislation, its power had been eclipsed in the meantime by that of the "neo-conservatives," a movement inspired and led by a group of former Trotskyite intellectuals, who proposed to combine a "Welfare-State" at home, also called "democratic capitalism," with US imperialism abroad and the drive toward world-domination. Under the influence of the "neo-cons," then, NATO was not only not abolished but further upgraded and expanded instead. Post-Soviet Russia was increasingly encircled by NATO troops, and the US attacked and waged war against one country after another — Afghanistan, Iraq, Libya, Serbia, Somalia, Sudan, Syria — orchestrated coups (Ukraine, Egypt), or imposed economic sanctions and blockades against other countries (Iran), for little more reason than their unwillingness to take orders from the neo-cons in charge of US foreign policy. The European Left, with its traditional anti-imperialist stance, should have been appalled and vigorously resisted these policies. But instead, through US economic pressure, threats and bribes, most (though not all) European parties of the Left swiftly relented and became willing accomplices in these imperialist endeavors. And this, by its own standards treacherous change in the policy of the European Left, then, would in turn lead to yet another momentous strategic twist in its agenda.

Whether intended or not, the result of US imperialism, the bloodshed, social turmoil, and economic devastation it caused, generated a continuously growing flood of people from the Balkans, the Near- and Middle East and northern Africa trying to make their way into the countries of democratic socialist Western

Europe. The national or "right" socialists, in accordance with general public sentiment, opposed and tried to resist this threat of an invasion by millions and millions of foreign "immigrants." The socialist Left on the other hand, taking a leaf from the US Left in this regard, perceived and portrayed mass immigration as an opportunity for another great leap forward in its egalitarian agenda and accordingly did little or nothing to prevent it or even promoted it. Regrettably, it would put downward pressure on domestic wages and thus endanger the support from its own traditional working-class voter base. More importantly, however, it would be instrumental in breaking up any and all resistance against the further centralization and concentration of socialist powers in the EU headquarters of Brussels, whether from national socialist forces or more radically and fundamentally from the side of right libertarians. Through a policy of "free immigration," in mixing, on the same territory, in immediate proximity, people of different nationalities, ethnicities, languages, cultures, customs, traditions and religions, of different histories, upbringings, value systems and mental makeups, increasing social fragmentation would result. All still existing personal affiliations other than those or even ranked above those to the central State and thus standing in the way of the further expansion of State power, i.e., affiliations to one's own nation, ethnicity, religion, region, town, community or family, would be systematically weakened. Everyone would be increasingly "equalized" in universal and ubiquitous dis-unity, social strife and conflict, and be equally left at the sole mercy of the all-mighty State and its socialist rulers. And to this end, then, every dissenter would have to be systematically

denounced by the dominant class of leftist intellectuals in the strongest possible terms, as some despicable
and vile outcast best to be forever silenced.

In the following, Lew Rockwell lays bare the horrifying progress that the socialists of all stripes, whether
of the "rightist" or the "leftist" kind, have made already
in the pursuit of their egalitarian agenda, and he draws
out the lessons to be learned from this for libertarians.

Introduction

AGAINST THE LEFT EXPLORES SOMETHING basic to libertarianism that many people today have forgotten. As everyone knows, libertarians view the State and the individual as fundamentally opposed. People who freely interact in the market create on their own a wonderful society that advances progress. The State, as Murray Rothbard explained, is a criminal gang of predators. It takes away what people produce, confiscating wealth for its own nefarious purposes.

So much is common knowledge, and in *Against the Left*, I show in detail how the State does this. What is often forgotten, though, is that libertarianism accepts people as they are. If we get rid of the State — and that is a big if — we have accomplished our goal as libertarians. Libertarianism does not try to remold people to make them conform to some supposedly desirable ideology. It does not embark on the futile quest of making everybody equal. It does not favor trying to end "discrimination". It does not view the traditional family as an enemy. To the contrary, it views the traditional family as the basis for a decent society.

Two great thinkers have taught us these truths better than anyone else: Ludwig von Mises and his foremost student, Murray N. Rothbard. Their insights are basic to this book.

Unfortunately, a number of so-called libertarians ignore these essential points. These left libertarians attempt the impossible. They want to combine libertarianism, with its polar opposite, egalitarianism. It's not enough for people to be libertarian. They must also be "nice," where this means surrendering to the latest leftist claptrap.

In *Against the Left*, we examine some key battlegrounds in the struggle to preserve and advance real libertarianism against its enemies. These include the assault on the family, civil rights and "disabilities," immigration, environmentalism, and economic egalitarianism. In the last chapter, we directly confront the left-libertarian impostors who want to take libertarianism away from us.

CHAPTER 1

The Assault
on the Family

TODAY, THE FUNDAMENTAL THREAT TO liberty comes from leftist programs to promote absolute equality. In this chapter, we will first describe egalitarianism in general terms and then discuss one of its main, and most dangerous, manifestations. This is the attempt to destroy the traditional family, the hallmark of civilization. The homosexual agenda demanding same-sex marriage, among many other revolutionary measures, and the feminist movement play a foremost role in this plot against the family.

In order to maintain a free society, it is essential that the traditional family, i.e., the union of one man and one woman in marriage, in most cases to raise a family, be preserved. Ludwig von Mises offers some profound insights on this matter.

In Chapter IV of Part I of *Socialism*, Mises points out something that left-libertarian opponents of the traditional family would do well to bear in mind. (But of course they won't.) The modern assault on the family stems from socialism:

> Proposals to transform the relations between the sexes have long gone hand in hand with plans for the socialization of the means of production. Marriage is to disappear along with private property, giving place to an arrangement more in harmony with the fundamental facts of sex. When man is liberated from the yoke of economic labour, love is to be liberated from all the economic trammels which have profaned it. Socialism promises not only welfare — wealth for all — but universal happiness in love as well.

Feminists and left-libertarians claim the family is oppressive, but in fact the bourgeois family saved women from oppression.

> As the idea of contract enters the Law of Marriage, it breaks the rule of the male, and makes the wife a partner with equal rights. From a one-sided relationship resting on force, marriage thus becomes a mutual agreement; the servant becomes the married wife entitled to demand from the man all that he is entitled to ask from her. Step by step she wins the position in the home which she holds today. Nowadays the position of the woman differs from the position of the man only in so far as their peculiar ways of earning a living differ. The remnants of man's privileges have little importance. They are privileges of honour. The wife, for instance, still bears her husband's name.

As Mises points out, women's position improved because of capitalist property relations. Far from being oppressive, as Marxists and other leftists contend, they liberated women:

> This evolution of marriage has taken place by way of the law relating to the property of married persons. Woman's position in marriage was improved as the principle of violence was thrust back, and as the idea of contract advanced in other fields of the Law of Property it necessarily transformed the property relations between the married couple. The wife was freed from the power of her husband for the first time when she gained legal rights over the wealth which she brought into marriage and which she acquired during marriage, and when that which her husband customarily gave her was transformed into allowances enforceable by law.

For Mises, the law of property under capitalism was all-embracing in its effects:

> Thus marriage, as we know it, has come into existence entirely as a result of the contractual idea penetrating into this sphere of life. All our cherished ideals of marriage have grown out of this idea. That marriage unites one man and one woman, that it can be entered into only with the free will of both parties, that it imposes a duty of mutual fidelity, that a man's violations of the marriage vows are to be judged no differently from a woman's, that the rights of husband and wife are essentially the same — these principles develop

from the contractual attitude to the problem of marital life. No people can boast that their ancestors thought of marriage as we think of it today. Science cannot judge whether morals were once more severe than they are now. We can establish only that our views of what marriage should be are different from the views of past generations and that their ideal of marriage seems immoral in our eyes.

Mises, it is clear, had no use for feminism. His view of the importance for women of having children would be anathema to today's feminists.

The radical wing of Feminism, which holds firmly to this standpoint, overlooks the fact that the expansion of woman's powers and abilities is inhibited not by marriage, not by being bound to man, children, and household, but by the more absorbing form in which the sexual function affects the female body. Pregnancy and the nursing of children claim the best years of a woman's life, the years in which a man may spend his energies in great achievements. One may believe that the unequal distribution of the burden of reproduction is an injustice of nature, or that it is unworthy of woman to be child-bearer and nurse, but to believe this does not alter the fact. It may be that a woman is able to choose between renouncing either the most profound womanly joy, the joy of motherhood, or the more masculine development of her personality in action and endeavour. It may be that she has no such choice. It may be that in suppressing her urge towards motherhood she does herself an injury that reacts through all other functions of her being. But whatever the truth about this, the fact remains that when she becomes a mother, with or without marriage, she is prevented from leading her life as freely and independently as man. Extraordinarily gifted women may achieve fine things in spite of motherhood; but because the functions of sex have the first claim upon woman, genius and the greatest achievements have been denied her.

Mises didn't oppose every aspect of feminism. So long as it confined itself to favoring equal rights, as understood by classical liberalism, it was fine:

So far as Feminism seeks to adjust the legal position of woman to that of man, so far as it seeks to offer her legal and economic freedom to develop and act in accordance with her inclinations, desires, and economic circumstances — so far it is nothing more than a branch of the great liberal movement, which advocates peaceful and free evolution. When, going beyond this, it attacks the institutions of social life under the impression that it will thus be able to remove the natural barriers, it is a spiritual child of Socialism. For it is a characteristic of Socialism to discover in social institutions the origin of unalterable facts of nature, and to endeavour, by reforming these institutions, to reform nature.

For Mises, the feminist drive to abolish the family rested on a total misconception of the place of women in society:

> The misconception to which the principle of equality before the law is exposed in the field of general social relationships is to be found in the special field of the relations between those sexes. Just as the pseudo-democratic movement endeavours by decrees to efface natural and socially conditioned inequalities, just as it wants to make the strong equal to the weak, the talented to the untalented, and the healthy to the sick, so the radical wing of the women's movement seeks to make women the equal of men. Though they cannot go so far as to shift half the burden of motherhood on to men, still they would like to abolish marriage and family life so that women may have at least all that liberty which seems compatible with childbearing. Unencumbered by husband and children, woman is to move freely, act freely, and live for herself and the development of her personality.

In order to grasp Mises's line of argument, we need to keep in mind a key point. Ignoring this point is the major failing of all leftists. Legal equality doesn't abolish biological differences. Thus, it doesn't follow from the fact that women don't earn as much as men, or don't hold as many powerful positions, that they are victims of discrimination:

> But difference between sexual character and sexual destiny can no more be decreed away than other inequalities of mankind. It is

not marriage which keeps woman inwardly unfree, but the fact that her sexual character demands surrender to a man and that her love for husband and children consumes her best energies. There is no human law to prevent the woman who looks for happiness in a career from renouncing love and marriage. But those who do not renounce them are not left with sufficient strength to master life as a man may master it. It is the fact that sex possesses her whole personality, and not the facts of marriage and family, which enchains woman. By "abolishing" marriage one would not make woman any freer and happier; one would merely take from her the essential content of her life, and one could offer nothing to replace it.

Woman's struggle to preserve her personality in marriage is part of that struggle for personal integrity which characterizes the rationalist society of the economic order based on private ownership of the means of production. It is not exclusively to the interest of woman that she should succeed in this struggle; to contrast the interests of men and women, as extreme feminists try to do, is very foolish. All mankind would suffer if woman should fail to develop her ego and be unable to unite with man as equal, freeborn companions and comrades.

To take away a woman's children and put them in an institution is to take away part of her life; and children are deprived of the most far-reaching influences when they are torn from the bosom of the family. Only recently Freud, with the insight of genius, has shown how deep are the impressions which the parental home leaves on the child. From the parents the child learns to love, and so comes to possess the forces which enable it to grow up into a healthy human being. The segregated educational institution breeds homosexuality and neurosis. It is no accident that the proposal to treat men and women as radically equal, to regulate sexual intercourse by the State, to put infants into public nursing homes at birth and to ensure that children and parents remain quite unknown to each other should have originated with Plato; he saw only the satisfaction of a physical craving in the relations between the sexes. The evolution which has led from the principle of violence to the contractual principle has based these relations on free choice in love. The woman may deny herself to anyone, she may demand fidelity and constancy from the man to whom she gives herself. Only in this way is the foundation laid for the development of woman's individuality. By returning to the principle of violence with a conscious neglect of the contractual idea, Socialism, even though it aims at an equal distribution of the plunder, must finally demand promiscuity in sexual life.

Mises, by the way, wasn't very favorable to homosexuals, though he didn't write much about the subject. But what he does say leaves no room for doubt about his un-PC attitude:

> Some kinds of work satisfy particular wishes. There are, for example, occupations which meet erotic desires — either conscious or subconscious ones. These desires may be normal or perverse. Also fetishists, homosexuals, sadists and other perverts can sometimes find in their work an opportunity to satisfy their strange appetites. There are occupations which are especially attractive to such people. Cruelty and blood-thirstiness luxuriantly thrive under various occupational cloaks.

It is sometimes argued that because libertarians want the state to get out of the marriage business — as it should out of every business — that the state ought to be neutral between regular marriage and same sex marriage. That is, if the state grants marriage licenses at all, which it shouldn't, then it ought to grant them indiscriminately to all who apply. Similarly, so long as a national army exists, women and gays should be admitted into the service on the same terms as men. The state, it is argued, cannot discriminate.

But this doesn't follow at all. Libertarianism is a theory of what people's rights should be. It rules out the state; and, to the unfortunate extent the state exists, libertarians hold that the state should, to the greatest extent possible, refrain from violating people's rights. Beyond this, libertarianism mandates nothing to the state. Libertarians don't have to hold that the state must grant marriage licenses to couples of the same sex.

Similarly, as Rothbard pointed out, the state isn't required to allow gays to serve in the armed forces.

> The military should be considered like any other business, organization, or service; its decisions should be based on what's best for the military and "rights" have nothing to do with such decisions. The military's long-standing ban on gays in the military has nothing to do with "rights" or even "homophobia"; rather it is the result of long experience as well as common sense. The military is not like any civilian organization. Not only are its men in combat situations (which it partially shares with civilian outfits like the police) but the military commander has virtual total control over his subordinate's person and life, especially in combat situations. In such situations, open homosexuals could engage in favoritism toward loved ones, and engage in sexual exploitation and abuse of subordinates under their command. Add the discomfort of many in close and intimate situations, and you get destruction of the morale and efficiency of combat units.

Rothbard acknowledged that gays had an answer to these claims, but he found it unacceptable.

> The standard answer of gays is interesting for being both abstract and unresponsive to the point. Namely: all sexual activities are and should be illegal in the military much

less sexual abuse of subordinates. Make only actions illegal say the advocates of gays in the military and make any orientation licit and legitimate. One problem with this libertarian-sounding answer is that it confuses what should be illegal per se from what should be illegal as a voluntary member of an organization (e.g., the military) which can and should have its own rules of membership, let alone its own hiring and promoting and firing. In criminal law, only actions (such as robbery and murder) should be illegal, and not mental orientation. But who should or should not be a member of the military should depend on military rules, and not simply include anyone who is not a criminal. Thus, frail types who are half-blind are clearly not in a per se state of criminality; but surely the military has the right to bar such people from membership.

Secondly, the standard pro-gay answer ignores the facts of human nature. Surely libertarians in particular should be alive to the absurdity of making sex illegal and then declaring an end to the matter. The point is that the military understands that, while sex in the military should indeed be outlawed, that this is not going to settle the matter, because human nature often triumphs over the law. Prostitution has been illegal from time immemorial, but it has scarcely disappeared. It is precisely because of its shrewd understanding of human nature that the military wants to keep the ban on gays in the military. The military doesn't naïvely assume that there are no gays in the army or navy now. On the other hand, it has no intention of going on a "witch hunt" to try to ferret out secret gays. The whole point is that, with gays necessarily in the closet, the problem of favoritism, sexual abuse, etc. is greatly minimized. Allow open gaydom in the military, however, and the problems, and the suffering of morale, will escalate. The same strictures apply a fortiori to women in the military, especially to integrated close-contact and intimate units such as exist in combat. (The old method of segregated female units for typing, jeep-driving, etc. did not pose such problems.) Since there are far more heterosexual than homosexual males, and since there is no question of a "closet" here, favoritism and abuse will be far more rampant. Once again, illegalizing sex within the military would be even more difficult to enforce. This is especially true in the current climate where "sexual harassment" has been expanded to touching and even ogling. Think of sex-integrated showers and think of Tailhook maximized to the nth degree! The problem of women in the military has been further aggravated by the sex-norming of physical requirements in the military. Since it proved almost impossible for women to pass the standard tests for strength and speed, these tests have been dumbed down so that most women can pass them; and this includes such essential combat skills as carrying weapons and throwing grenades!

We've already noted that libertarianism doesn't mandate that the state treat all groups equally. Unfortunately, left libertarians disagree. Rothbard answered them in this way:

> Finally, libertarians will fall back on their standard argument that while all these strictures do apply to private organizations, and that "rights" do not apply to such organizations, egalitarian rights do apply to such governmental outfits as the military: But, as I have written in the case of whether someone has "the right" to stink up a public library just because it is public, this sort of nihilism has to be abandoned. I'm in favor of privatizing everything, but short of that glorious day, existing government services should be operated as efficiently as possible. Surely, the postal service should be privatized, but, pending that happy day should we advocate allowing postal workers to toss all the mail into the dumpster, in the name of making that service as terrible as possible? Apart from the horrors such a position would impose upon the poor consumers (that's us), there is another grave error to this standard libertarian position (which I confess I once held), that it besmirches and confuses the fair concept of "rights," and transmutes it from a strict defense of an individual's person and property to a confused, egalitarian mishmash. Hence, "anti-discrimination" or

even affirmative action "rights" in public services sets the conditions for their admittedly monstrous expansion into the private realm.

He elaborated on this vital point on another occasion:

All of libertarian political thought follows from the non-aggression principle: that no one, including the government, can aggress against someone else's person or property. Since according to libertarian theory; there should be no government property since it is all derived from coercion, how does any principle whatever of government property use follow from libertarian theory? The answer is, it doesn't. On the question of what to do about government property, libertarians, apart from calling for privatization, are set adrift, in short, with nothing but their common sense and their attunement to the real world, of which libertarians have always been in notoriously short supply.

But if Rothbard is right that the state doesn't have to recognize same sex marriage or promote the gay and feminist agendas, why shouldn't it? Here again, we can look to Rothbard for the answer. He characterized feminism in this way:

Men are the evil, victimizer sex; women are the good, victimized sex. The two genders are ineluctable enemies. Therefore, all tactics and strategies are permissible and valuable if they result in the victory of women over the Male Enemy. Hence, attack one-sex colleges if they are male, proclaim their greatness if they are female. If you are talking about qualities such as career advancement, intelligence, success, proclaim women as exactly man's equal and denounce as "sexist" any intimation to the contrary; but if you are talking about such good things as nurturing, peace, etc., proclaim women's innate superiority. Don't worry about such "objective" qualities as fairness, logic, truth, or non-contradiction; remember, all's fair in hate and war.

In this regard, all accusations that a man has sexually harassed a woman are automatically given credence:

> The basic premise of the Regiment, always implicit, sometimes explicit, is that whenever any woman whatsoever makes a charge of "sexual harassment" (or date rape, or rape, or whatever), that the charge must be taken by everyone as per se true. Any doubt expressed, let alone any challenge to try to impeach the witness, is considered per se evil, an attempt to blame or once again "harass" the "victim." Note that this truly monstrous view can only make sense if one holds as a basic axiom that any woman's charge must always be treated as gospel truth.

Feminists often respond to criticism of the sort Rothbard gives by saying that "you just don't get it." Rothbard had a devastating answer:

> There are two successful and powerful rebuttals to be made to the "you men just don't get

it" charge. One is: no, ladies, *You* don't get it: you don't get the crucial distinction between harmless verbal flirting, verbal threats of job loss in demanding sexual favors, and physical assault. We don't "get" the continuum thesis because that thesis is evil and wrong, and for reasons we have just outlined. The second rebuttal is to turn the "you just don't get it" thesis on its head. Look, ladies, women, womyn, viragos, or what you will: you seem to be claiming that since we are men, we can't possibly get it, that only women can reach this magic realm of understanding. You are engaging in the fallacy of what Ludwig von Mises called "polylogism." But let's assume for the sake of argument that you are right. But in that case, why do you keep talking? If men and women are doomed to see the issue totally differently, then it is hopeless to try to convince us. And therefore, why don't you just shut up?

But of course women don't want to shut up, because the whole point of this "you just don't get it" ploy is to browbeat men into shutting up, and into going along with this nonsense even though they are unconvinced. To go along, and to grant organized womanhood permanent victim status, with all the goodies in power, perks, and income that such status implies.

From the viewpoint of libertarian theory, Rothbard pointed out, the feminist agenda is nonsense:

Here, libertarian doctrine comports totally with old-fashioned law, that is law before the civil rights hokum came onto the books. Very simply; there ain't no such crime as "sexual harassment." Physical assault or rape has been considered a crime from time immemorial, and it still is. There is no need for some extra "crime" called S.H. To prosecute such a crime, there is no need for special administrative bureaus or commissions. The start of the evil can be pinpointed precisely: the monstrous Civil Rights Act of 1964, specifically Title VII, prohibited discrimination in employment on the basis of race, religion, sex, and other possible characteristics. This horrendous invasion of the property rights of the employer is the source of all the rest of the ills, neocons and sellout Libertarians to the contrary notwithstanding. If I am an employer and, for whatever reason, I wish to hire only five-foot-four albinos. I should have the absolute right to do so. Period.

Rothbard extended his criticism to cover the full range of the feminist movement:

It is high time, and past due, that someone blew the whistle on "Women's Liberation." Like The Environment, Women's Lib is suddenly and raucously everywhere in the last few months. It has become impossible to avoid being assaulted, day in and day out, by the noisy blather of the Women's Movement. Special issues of magazines, TV news programs, and newspapers have been devoted to this new-found "problem"; and nearly two dozen books on women's lib are being scheduled for publication this year by major publishers.

Rothbard pointed out that almost all the books and articles about feminism favor the movement, a situation that continues to the present. He found this state of affairs deplorable.

> In all this welter of verbiage, not one article, not one book, not one program has dared to present the opposition case. The injustice of this one-sided tidal wave should be evident. Not only is it evident, but the lack of published opposition negates one of the major charges of the women's lib forces: that the society and economy are groaning under a monolithic male "sexist" tyranny. If the men are running the show, how is it that they do not even presume to print or present anyone from the other side?

> Yet the "oppressors" remain strangely silent, which leads one to suspect, as we will develop further below, that perhaps the "oppression" is on the other side.

Rothbard viewed with contempt the weak male responses to feminism.

> In the meanwhile, the male "oppressors" are acting, in the manner of Liberals everywhere, like scared, or guilt-ridden, rabbits. When the one hundred viragos of Women's Lib bullied their way into the head offices of the *Ladies' Home Journal*, did the harried editor-in-chief, John Mack Carter, throw these aggressors

out on their collective ear, as he should have done? Did he, at the very least, abandon his office for the day and go home? No, instead he sat patiently for eleven hours while these harridans heaped abuse upon him and his magazine and his gender, and then meekly agreed to donate to them a special section of the *Journal*, along with $10,000 ransom. In this way, spineless male Liberalism meekly feeds the appetite of the aggressors and paves the way for the next set of outrageous "demands." *Rat* magazine, an underground tabloid, caved in even more spectacularly, and simply allowed itself to be taken over permanently by a "women's liberation collective."

But this account of feminism leaves us with a problem. If it's such a weird, and bad, movement, how did it ever manage to gain a foothold? Once more, Rothbard has the answer:

Why, in fact, this sudden upsurge of women's lib? Even the most fanatic virago of the Women's Movement concedes that this new movement has not emerged in response to any sudden clamping down of the male boot upon the collective sensibilities of the American female. Instead, the new uprising is part of the current degeneracy of the New Left, which, as its one-time partly libertarian politics and ideology and organization have collapsed, has been splintering into absurd and febrile forms, from Maoism to Weathermanship to mad bombings to women's lib. The heady wine of "liberation" for every crackpot group has been in the air for some time, sometimes deserved but more often absurd, and now the New Left women have gotten into the act. We need not go quite so far as the recent comment of Professor Edward A. Shils, eminent sociologist at the University of Chicago, that he now expects a "dog liberation front," but it is hard to fault the annoyance behind his remark. Throughout the whole gamut of "liberation," the major target has been the harmless, hard-working, adult WASP American male, William Graham Sumner's Forgotten Man; and now this hapless Dagwood Bumstead figure is being battered yet once more. How long will it be before the put-upon, long-suffering Average American at last loses his patience, and rises up in his wrath to do some effective noise-making on his own behalf?

We have said a lot about the feminist movement, but what exactly is it? How did it come about?

The current Women's Movement is divisible into two parts. The older, slightly less irrational wing began in 1963 with the publication of Betty Friedan's *The Feminine Mystique* and her organization of NOW (the National Organization of Women). NOW concentrates on alleged economic discrimination against women. For example: the point that while the median annual wage for all jobs in 1968 was almost $7700 for men, it only totaled $4500 for women, 58% of the male figure. The other major point is the quota argument: that if one casts one's eye about various professions, top management positions, etc., the quota of women is far lower than their supposedly deserved 51%, their share of the total population.

Rothbard destroyed the quota argument:

The quota argument may be disposed of rapidly; for it is a two-edged sword. If the low percentage of women in surgery, law, management, etc., is proof that the men should posthaste be replaced by females, then what are we to do with the Jews, for example, who shine far above their assigned quota in the professions, in medicine, in academia, etc.? Are they to be purged?

Even if quotas can't be accepted, what about the feminist point that women earn less than men?

The lower average income for women can be explained on several grounds, none of which involve irrational "sexist" discrimination. One is the fact that the overwhelming majority of women work a few years, and then take a large chunk of their productive years to raise children, after which they may or may not decide to return to the labor force. As a result, they tend to enter, or to find, jobs largely in those industries and in that type of work that does not require a long-term commitment to a career. Furthermore, they tend to find jobs in those occupations where the cost of training new people, or of losing old ones, is relatively low.

These tend to be lower-paying occupations than those that require a long-term commitment or where costs of training or turnover are high. This general tendency to take out years for child-raising also accounts for a good deal of the failure to promote women to higher-ranking, and therefore higher-paying jobs, and hence for the low female "quotas" in these areas. It is easy to hire secretaries who do not intend to make the job their continuing life work; it is not so easy to promote people up the academic or the corporate ladder who do not do so. How does a dropout for motherhood get to be a corporate president or a full professor?

But there is a deeper issue, definitely an "un-PC one;" and Rothbard faced it head on:

While these considerations account for a good chunk of lower pay and lower ranked jobs for women, they do not fully explain the problem. In the capitalist market economy, women have full freedom of opportunity; irrational discrimination in employment tends to be minimal in the free market, for the simple reason that the employer also suffers from such discriminatory practice. In the free market, every worker tends to earn the value of his product, his "marginal productivity." Similarly, everyone tends to fill the job he can best accomplish, to work at his most productive efforts. Employers who persist in paying below a person's marginal product will hurt themselves by losing their best workers and hence losing profits for themselves. If women have persistently lower pay and poorer jobs, even after correcting for the motherhood-dropout, then the simple reason must be that their marginal productivity tends to be lower than men.

It isn't surprising that Rothbard emphasized something that, as we've seen, Mises also emphasized. These great minds usually thought alike:

It should be emphasized that, in contrast to the Women's Lib forces who tend to blame capitalism as well as male tyrants for centuries-old discrimination, it was precisely capitalism and the "capitalist revolution" of the 18th and 19th centuries that freed women from male oppression, and set each woman free to find her best level. It was the feudal and pre-capitalist, pre-market society that was marked by male oppression; it was that society where women were chattels of their fathers and husbands, where they could own no property of their own, etc. Capitalism set women free to find their own level, and the result is what we have today.

The Women Libs retort that women possess the full potential of equality of output and productivity with men, but that they have been browbeaten during centuries of male oppression. But the conspicuous lack of rising to the highest posts under capitalism still remains. There are few women doctors, for example. Yet medical schools nowadays not only don't discriminate against women, they bend over backwards to accept them (i.e., they discriminate in their favor); yet the proportion of women doctors is still not noticeably high.

Naturally, the feminists didn't accept reality when it contradicted their fantasies:

Here the female militants fall back on another argument: that centuries of being "brainwashed" by a male-dominated culture have made most women passive, accepting their allegedly inferior role, and even liking and enjoying their major role as homemakers and child-raisers. And the real problem for the raucous females, of course, is that the overwhelming majority of women do embrace the "feminine mystique," do feel that their sole careers are those of housewife and mother. Simply to write off these evident and strong desires by most women as "brainwashing" proves far too much; for we can always dismiss any person's values, no matter how deeply held, as the result of "brainwashing." The "brainwashing" contention becomes what the philosophers call "operationally meaningless," for it means that the female militants refuse to accept any evidence, logical or empirical, of whatever kind, that might prove their contentions to be wrong. Show them a woman who loves domesticity and they dismiss this as "brainwashing"; show them a militant and they claim that this proves that women are yearning for "liberation." In short, these militants regard their flimsy contentions as unworthy of any sort of proof; but this is the groundless method of mystics rather than an argument reflecting scientific truth.

And so the high rate of conversion claimed by women's liberationists proves nothing either; may not this be the result of "brain-washing" by the female militants? After all, if you are a redhead, and a Redheaded Liberation League suddenly emerges and shouts at you that you are eternally oppressed by vile nonredheads, some of you might well join in the fray. Which proves nothing at all about whether or not redheads are objectively oppressed.

Rothbard didn't contend that women shouldn't have a career.

I do not go so far as the extreme male "sexists" who contend that women should confine themselves to home and children, and that any search for alternative careers is unnatural. On the other hand, I do not see much more support for the opposite contention that domestic-type women are violating their natures. There is in this as in all matters a division of labor, and in a free market society every individual will enter those fields and areas of work which he or she finds most attractive. The proportion of working women is far higher than even 20 years ago, and that is fine; but it is still a minority of females, and that's fine too. Who are you or I to tell anyone, male or female, what occupation he or she should enter?

Furthermore, the women libs have fallen into a logical trap in their charge of centuries of male brainwashing. For if this charge be true, then how come that men have been running the culture over eons of time? Surely, this cannot be an accident. Isn't this evidence of male superiority?

Unfortunately, these feminists are the "moderates." There is an even more outrageous position:

The Friedanites, [followers of Betty Friedan] who call stridently for equality of income and position, have, however, been outpaced in recent months by the more militant women's liberationists, or "new feminists," women who work with the older movement but consider them conservative "Aunt Toms." These new militants, who have been getting most of the publicity, persistently liken their alleged oppression to that of blacks, and like the black movement reject equality and integration for a radical change in society. They call for the revolutionary abolition of alleged male rule and its supposed corollary, the family. Displaying a deep-seated and scarcely concealed hatred of men per se, these females call for all-women's communes, state-run children, test-tube babies, or just simply the "cutting up of men," as the real founder of militant women's lib, Valerie Solanis, put it in her

SCUM (Society for Cutting Up Men) Manifesto. Solanis became the culture-heroine of the New Feminism in 1968 when she shot and almost killed the painter and filmmaker Andy Warhol. Instead of being dismissed (as she would be by any rational person) as a lone nut, the liberated females wrote articles praising Solanis as the "sweet assassin" who tried to dispose of the "plastic male" Warhol. We should have known at that point of the travails that lay in store.

Rothbard reverses the claim of the extreme feminists. Far from men dominating women, it is much more frequent that women dominate men.

I believe that modern American marriages are, by and large, conducted on a basis of equality, but I also believe that the opposite contention is far closer to the truth than that of the New Feminists: namely, that it is men, not women, who are more likely to be the oppressed class, or gender, in our society, and that it is far more the men who are the "blacks," the slaves, and women their masters. In the first place, the female militants claim that marriage is a diabolical institution by which husbands enslave their wives and force them to rear children and do housework. But let us consider: in the great majority of the cases, who is it that insists on marriage, the man or the woman? Everyone knows the answer. And if this great desire for marriage is the result of male brainwashing, as the Women's Libs contend, then how is it that so many men resist marriage, resist this prospect of their lifelong seat upon the throne of domestic "tyranny"?

Indeed, as capitalism has immensely lightened the burden of housework through improved technology, many wives have increasingly constituted a kept leisure class. In the middle class neighborhood in which I live, I see them, these "oppressed" and hard-faced viragos, strutting down the street in their mink stoles to the next bridge or mahjongg game, while their husbands are working themselves into an early coronary down in the garment district to support their helpmeets.

Rothbard drew an important parallel with the history of the American South.

In these cases, then, who are the "niggers": the wives? Or the husbands? The women's libs claim that men are the masters because they are doing most of the world's work. But if we look back at the society of the slave South, who indeed did the work? It is always the slaves who do the work, while the masters live in relative idleness off the fruits of their labor. To the extent that husbands work and support the family, while wives enjoy a kept status, who then are the masters?

Rothbard returned to the attack on female domination:

There is nothing new in this argument, but it is a point that has been forgotten amidst the current furor. It has been noted for years — and especially by Europeans and Asians — that too many American men live in a matriarchy, dominated first by Momism, then by female teachers, and then by their wives. Blondie and Dagwood have long symbolized for sociologists an all-too prevalent American matriarchy, a matriarchy that contrasts to the European scene where the women, though more idle than in the U.S., do not run the home. The henpecked American male has long been the butt of perceptive humor. And, finally, when the male dies, as he usually does, earlier than his spouse, she inherits the entire family assets, with the result that far more than 50% of the wealth of America is owned by women. Income — the index of hard and productive work — is less significant here than ownership of ultimate wealth. Here is another inconvenient fact which the female militants brusquely dismiss as of no consequence. And, finally, if the husband should seek a divorce, he is socked with the laws of alimony, which he is forced to pay and pay to support a female whom he no longer sees, and, if he fails to pay, faces the barbaric penalty of imprisonment — the only instance remaining in our legal structure of imprisonment for nonpayment of "debt." Except, of course, that this is a "debt" which the man had never voluntarily incurred. Who, then, are the slaves?

And as for men forcing women to bear and rear children, who, again, in the vast majority of cases, is the party in the marriage most eager to have children? Again, everyone knows the answer.

The feminists tried to respond to this argument, but their answer was weak:

When, as they do at times, the female militants acknowledge matriarchal dominance by the American female, their defense, as usual, is to fall back on the operationally meaningless: that the seeming dominance of the wife is only the reflection of her quintessential passivity and subordination, so that women have to seek various roads to bitchiness and manipulation as their route to ... power. Beneath their seeming power, then, these wives are psychologically unhappy. Perhaps, but I suppose that one could argue that the slavemaster in the Old South was also psychologically uneasy because of his unnaturally dominant role. But the politico-economic fact of his dominance remained, and this is the major point.

The ultimate test of whether women are enslaved or not in the modem marriage is the one of "natural law": to consider what would happen if indeed the women's libs had their way and there were no marriage. In that situation, and in a consequently promiscuous world, what would happen to the children? The answer is that the only visible and demonstrable parent would be the mother. Only the mother would have the child, and therefore only the mother would be stuck with the child. In short, the women militants who complain that they are stuck with the task of raising the children should heed the fact that, in a world without marriage, they would also be stuck with the task of earning all of the income for their children's support. I suggest that they contemplate this prospect long and hard before they continue to clamor for the abolition of marriage and the family.

A central theme of this book is the importance of the traditional family for preserving our liberty and civilization. Unless we can pass on our heritage to our children, we are doomed. Feminists cannot handle this vital problem, as Rothbard noted:

The more thoughtful of the female militants have recognized that their critical problem is finding a solution for the raising of children. Who is going to do it? The moderates answer: governmental provision of day-care centers, so that women can be freed to enter the labor force. But the problem here, aside from the general problem of socialism or statism, is this: how come that the free market hasn't provided day care centers fairly inexpensively, as it does for any product or service in mass demand? No one has to clamor for government provision of motels, for example. There are plenty of them. The economist is compelled to answer: either that the demand for mothers to go to work is not nearly as great as the New Feminists would have us believe, and/or some controls by government — perhaps requirements for registered nurses or licensing laws — are artificially restricting the supply. Whichever reason, then, more government is clearly not the answer.

Just as Mises pointed out that the failure of economic intervention leads to more radical interventions designed to "correct" the problems of the initial intervention, so are the radical feminists pushed to more and more extreme proposals. As Rothbard notes,

The more radical feminists are not content with such a piddling solution as day-care centers (besides who but women, other women this time, would be staffing these centers?). What they want, as Susan Brown-miller indicates in her *New York Sunday Times Magazine* article (March 15), is total husband-wife equality in all things, which means equally shared careers, equally shared housework, and equally shared child-rearing. Brownmiller recognizes that this would have to mean either that the husband works for six months and the wife for the next six months, with each alternating six months of child rearing, or that each work half of every day and so alternate the child-rearing each half-day. Whichever path is chosen, it is all too clear that this total equality could only be pursued if both parties are willing to live permanently on a hippie, subsistence, part-time-job level. For what career of any importance or quality can be pursued in such a fleeting and haphazard manner? Above the hippie level, then, this alleged "solution" is simply absurd.

If our analysis is correct, and we are already living in a matriarchy, then the true significance of the new feminism is not, as they would so stridently have it, the "liberation" of women from their oppression. May we not say that, not content with kept idleness and subtle domination, these women are reaching eagerly for total power? Not content with being supported and secure, they are now attempting to force their passive and long-suffering husbands to do most of the housework and childrearing as well. I know personally several couples where the wife is a militant liberationist and the husband has been brainwashed by his spouse to be an Uncle Tom and a traitor to his gender. In all these cases, after a long hard day at the office or at teaching to support the family, the husband sits at home tending the kids while the wife is out at Women's Lib meetings, there to plot their accession to total power and to denounce their husbands as sexist oppressors. Not content with the traditional mahjongg set, the New Woman is reaching for the final castrating blow — to be accepted, I suppose, with meek gratitude by their male-liberal spouses.

There is still the extremist women's lib solution: to abandon sex, or rather heterosexuality, altogether. There is no question but that this at least would solve the child-rearing problem. The charge of Lesbianism used to be considered a venomous male-chauvinist smear against the liberated woman. But in the burgeoning writings of the New Feminists there has run an open and increasing call for female homosexuality. Note, for example, Rita Mae Brown, writing in the first "liberated" issue of *Rat* (February 6):

"For a woman to vocally assert her heterosexuality is to emphasize her 'goodness' by her sexual activity with men. That old sexist brainwashing runs deep even into the consciousness of the most ardent feminist who will quickly tell you she loves sleeping with men. In fact, the worst thing you can call a woman in our society is a lesbian. Women are so male identified that they quake at the mention of this three-syllable word. The lesbian is, of course, the woman who has no need of men. When you think about it, what is so terrible about two women loving each other? To the insecure male, this is the supreme offense, the most outrageous blasphemy committed against the sacred scrotum.

After all, just what would happen if we all wound up loving each other. Good things for us but it would mean each man would lose his personal 'nigger' ... a real and great loss if you are a man. ...

To love another woman is an acceptance of sex which is a severe violation of the male culture (sex as exploitation) and therefore carries severe penalties. ... Women have been taught to abdicate the power of our bodies, both physically in athletics and self-defense, and sexually. To sleep with another woman is to confront the beauty and power of your own body as well as hers. You confront the experience of your sexual self-knowledge. You also confront another human being without the protective device of role. This may be too painful for most women as many have been so brutalized by heterosexual role play that they cannot begin to comprehend this real power. It is an overwhelming experience. I vulgarize it when I call it a freedom high. No wonder there is such resistance to lesbianism."

Or this, in the same issue, by "A. Weatherwoman":

Sex becomes entirely different without jealousy. Women who never saw themselves making it with women began digging each other sexually. ... What weatherman is doing is creating new standards for men and women to relate to. We are trying to make sex nonexploitative. ... We are making something new, with the common denominator being the revolution.

Or, finally, still in the same issue, by Robin Morgan:

> Let it all hang out. Let it seem bitchy, catty,
> dykey, frustrated, crazy, Solanisesque, nutty,
> frigid, ridiculous, bitter, embarrassing, man-
> hating, libelous. ... Sexism is not the fault of
> women — kill your fathers, not your moth-
> ers.

And so, at the hard inner core of the Women's Liberation Movement lies a bitter, extremely neurotic if not
psychotic, man-hating lesbianism. The quintessence of
the New Feminism is revealed.

Rothbard, as always, considered and refuted possible objections to his analysis:

> Is this spirit confined to a few extremists? Is
> it unfair to tar the whole movement with the
> brush of the Lesbian Rampant? I'm afraid
> not. For example, one motif now permeating
> the entire movement is a strident opposi-
> tion to men treating women as "sex objects."
> This supposedly demeaning, debasing, and
> exploitative treatment extends from pornog-
> raphy to beauty contests, to advertisements
> of pretty models using a product, all the way
> to wolf whistles and admiring glances at
> girls in miniskirts. But surely the attack on
> women as "sex objects" is simply an attack on
> sex, period, or rather, on hetero-sex. These
> new monsters of the female gender are out
> to destroy the lovely and age-old custom —
> delighted in by normal women the world
> over — of women dressing to attract men and
> succeeding at this pleasant task. What a dull
> and dreary world these termagants would
> impose upon us! A world where all girls look

like unkempt wrestlers, where beauty and attractiveness have been replaced by ugliness and "unisex," where delightful femininity has been abolished on behalf of raucous, aggressive, and masculine feminism.

Jealousy of pretty and attractive girls does, in fact, lie close to the heart of this ugly movement. One point that should be noted, for example, in the alleged economic discrimination against women: the fantastic upward mobility, as well as high incomes, available to the strikingly pretty girl. The Women's Libs may claim that models are exploited, but if we consider the enormous pay that the models enjoy — as well as their access to the glamorous life — and compare it with their opportunity cost foregone in other occupations such as waitress or typist — the charge of exploitation is laughable indeed. Male models, whose income and opportunities are far lower than that of females, might well envy the privileged female position! Furthermore, the potential for upward mobility for pretty, lower class girls is enormous, infinitely more so than for lower-class men: We might cite Bobo Rockefeller and Gregg Sherwood Dodge (a former pin-up model who married the multimillionaire scion of the Dodge family) as merely conspicuous examples. But these cases, far from counting as an argument against them, arouse the female liberationists to still greater fury, since one of their real complaints is against those more attractive girls who by virtue of their attractiveness, have been more successful in the inevitable competition for men — a competition that must exist whatever the form of government or society (provided, of course, that it remains heterosexual).

Women as "sex objects"? Of course they are sex objects, and praise the Lord they always will be. (Just as men, of course, are sex objects to women.) As for wolf whistles, it is impossible for any meaningful relationship to be established on the street or by looking at ads, and so in these roles women properly remain solely as sex objects. When deeper relationships are established between men and women, they each become more than sex objects to each other; they each hopefully become love objects as well. It would seem banal even to bother mentioning this, but in today's increasingly degenerate intellectual climate no simple truths can any longer be taken for granted. Contrast to the strident Women's Liberationists the charming letter in the *New York Sunday Times* (March '19) by Susan L. Peck, commenting on the Brownmiller article. After asserting that she, for one, welcomes male admiration, Mrs. Peck states that "To some this might sound square, but I do not harbor a mad, vindictive desire to see my already hard-working, responsible husband doing the household ironing." After decrying the female maladjustment exhibited in the "liberation movement," Mrs. Peck concludes:

"I, for one, adore men and I'd rather see than be one!" Hooray, and hopefully Mrs. Peck speaks for the Silent Majority of American womanhood.

As for the Women's Liberationists, perhaps we might begin to take their constantly repeated analogies with the black movement more seriously. The blacks have, indeed, moved from integration to black power, but the logic of black power is starkly and simply: black nationalism — an independent black nation. If our New Feminists wish to abandon male-female "integrationism" for liberation, then this logically implies Female Power, in short, Female Nationalism. Shall we then turn over some Virgin land, maybe the Black Hills, maybe Arizona, to these termagants? Yes, let them set up their karate-chopping Amazonian Women's Democratic People's Republic, and ban access to them. The infection of their sick attitudes and ideology would then be isolated and removed from the greater social body, and the rest of us, dedicated to good old-fashioned heterosexuality, could then go about our business undisturbed. It is high time that we heed the ringing injunction of William Butler Yeats:

"Down the fanatic, down the clown; Down, down, hammer them down," and that we echo the joyous cry of the elderly Frenchman in the famous joke. As a female militant in France addressed a gathering on women's liberation, asserting, "There is only a very small difference between men and women," the elderly Frenchman leaped to his feet, shouting, "Vive la petite difference!"

CHAPTER 2

"Civil Rights" and Disabilities

Rothbard deepened his attack, taking on the entire civil rights movement.

> On the entire question of legally and judicially imposed "civil rights," we have been subjected to a trap, to a shell game in which "both sides" adopt the same pernicious axiom and simply quarrel about interpretation within the same framework. On the one side, left-liberalism, which in the name of equality and civil rights, wants to outlaw "discrimination" everywhere, has pushed the process to the point of virtually mandating representational quotas for allegedly oppressed groups everywhere in the society; be it jobs and promotions, entry into private golf clubs, or in legislatures and among the judiciary. But the Official Conservative opposition, which includes not only neocons but also regular conservatives, conservative legal

foundations, and left-libertarians, adopts the self-same axiom of civil rights and equality. In the name of the alleged "original" civil rights vision of Martin Luther King, conservatives also want to outlaw discrimination in jobs and housing, and to allow federal courts to mandate gerrymandering of electoral districts. But while Official Conservatives fully endorse outlawing racial and other discrimination, they want to stop there, and claim that going beyond that to mandating affirmative action measures and quotas is perverting the noble original civil rights ideal.

The original sin of "civil rights," which would have been perfectly understood by such "old conservatives" as the much maligned Nine Old Men who tried to block the measures of the New Deal, is that anti-discrimination laws or edicts of any sort are evil because they run roughshod over the only fundamental natural right: the right of everyone over his own property. Every property owner should have the absolute right to sell, hire, or lease his money or other property to anyone whom he chooses, which means he has the absolute right to "discriminate" all he damn pleases. If I have a plant and want to hire only six-foot albinos, and I can find willing employees, I should have the right to do so, even though I might well lose my shirt doing so. (Of course I should not have the right to force the taxpayers to bail me out after losing my shirt.) If I own an apartment complex and want to rent only to Swedes without children, I should have the right to do so. Etc. Outlawing such discrimination, and restrictive covenants upholding it, was the original sin from which all other problems have flowed. Once admit that principle, and everything else follows as the night the day: Once concede that it is right to make it illegal for me to refuse to hire blacks (or substitute any other group, ethnic or gender or whatever you wish), then left-liberalism is far more logical than official conservatism. For if it is right and proper to outlaw my discriminating against blacks, then it is just as right and proper for the government to figure out if I am discriminating or not, and in that case, it is perfectly legitimate for them to employ quotas to test the proposition. Current conservatives say it is OK to outlaw discrimination if such a result is intended by employers or landlords, but that it is monstrous and illegitimate for the government to use statistics and other objective measures to figure out whether discrimination exists. Hence the spectre of quotas. But how can we figure out anyone else's subjective intent anyway? Given the premise of outlawing discrimination, then mandatory quotas, despite the undoubted horrors they bring in their wake, make perfect sense. It is not "going too far" that causes the trouble. The problem is not the abuse of the anti-discrimination axiom; the problem is the axiom itself. Nothing will help except challenging the basic axiom and reversing the "civil rights" revolution. Libertarians and conservatives who have any spunk left must drop their blinders and call not for "the original King equality" or the original civil rights ideal, but for throwing over the entire structure and restoring the absolute right of private property. "Freedom" must mean the freedom to discriminate.

Economies tank for big reasons and small, but usually both. The 2003 stagnation was prompted by investment imbalances created in the late 1990s that needed to be liquidated. But it was made worse by a thousand bad policies, some of which are being added by those seeking to "stimulate the economy," but not knowing how; others have long been on the books.

Consider: the government reports that job discrimination complaints against private employers increased 4 percent in 2002, to a total of 84,442, the highest level in seven years. Those filing complaints took in $310.5 million in monetary benefits. The main complaint involves race, followed by sex, but the big increase came with allegations involving religion, age, and national origin. The trend represents a huge diversion from the main goal of restoring economic growth.

The numbers themselves come nowhere near capturing the colossal costs associated with the laws that make this litigation possible. Every employer must constantly prepare and organize to diminish the likelihood that a complaint will be filed. In doing so, they take steps that lead to inefficiencies or avoid steps that might improve efficiency. Also, consider the costs imposed by those who threatened to file and did not because the issue was settled informally. Then consider the vast drain in human energy spent actually litigating these complaints (the typical case takes half a year to settle).

Hardly anyone is willing to talk about what these numbers really symbolize: a massive attack on freedom and free enterprise. The preeminent issue is property rights, the foundation of liberty and prosperity. The employee has no legitimate ownership over the property seized in the course of a complaint. His only legitimate ownership is over the contractually agreed-upon wage or income stream due him in the course of providing agreed-upon labor services. To the extent an employee grabs more than that, it is nothing more than theft under the cover of law.

In practice, discrimination law limits the freedom of property owners to use their money as they see fit. To understand this, we need to conceive of the employment contract as an exchange like any other. One person agrees to perform certain services and the party with whom he is making an exchange agrees to surrender a certain amount of his property in exchange for such services.

The contractual nature of the exchange is no different from a consumer's purchase of a gallon of milk from the store. The parties to the exchange agree on a voluntary basis to certain terms. To file a discrimination complaint is like going back to the store with a dagger (symbolizing the labor regulators at the EEOC) and demanding a retroactive price cut. Imagine if every store owner saw every customer as a person who has the potential of doing this legally, and you begin to understand how antidiscrimination law rattles the labor market.

The implied assumption behind all these laws is the idea that judges and bureaucrats can discover the real motivation behind every hiring, firing, or labor-management decision. It further assumes that the basis of all decisions taken in the workplace can be reduced to a simple form such as: I will not promote this person because she is a woman, too old, too non-religious, etc.

Everyone knows that decisions concerning the labor force seldom work this way. It's possible, of course, that a manager has a bias of a certain kind, but the nature of the marketplace is precisely to punish irrational biases with losses and reward objective decision-making with profits. It is for this reason that in a free market in the long run, good workers of any race, age, sex, or religion are rewarded for their virtues, while bad workers of all kinds are punished.

In practice, of course, bureaucrats do not actually feel the need to demonstrate that they have discovered the secrets of the human heart. What they do is assume certain motivations based on looking at overall patterns within the workplace. If women are generally earning less than men, for whatever reason (and there can be a million reasons unrelated to irrational bias), the burden of proof is on the employer to show that sex is not a consideration.

Ironically, the best way to demonstrate this is to adopt an opposite bias in favor of the criterion in question where necessary, and otherwise avoid, when possible, people who might file a successful complaint. For this reason, a law that forbids, say, race discrimination yields perverse results. People already hired from the known class of racial victims are likely to earn more than they otherwise would, even as new members of that group are less likely to be hired in the first place, precisely because they are more expensive than their expected labor inputs can justify.

Through this complicated economic, legal, and sociological process, we get *de facto* quotas, subsidized wages, gaps of unemployment, and a huge range of odd labor-market distortions. Such distortions can be absorbed in boom times, but they can make the difference between profits and bankruptcy in recessionary times like our own.

That is why the practices symbolized by the EEOC numbers hinder our prospects for recovery. Like protectionism, high taxes, deficits, massive government spending, and every other form of intervention in the free market, antidiscrimination law impedes the recovery that we desperately need. Business needs the freedom to manage its labor force according to its own lights right now. It does not need to spend its time and money dealing with DC discrimination bureaucrats.

In 1917, at the turn of the century, hotel entrepreneur Ellsworth M. Statler issued an instruction to his managers. It said:

> From this date you are instructed to employ only good-natured people, cheerful and pleasant, who smile easily and often. This ought to go for every job in the house. ... If it's necessary to clean house, do it. Don't protest. Get rid of the grouches, and the people that can't keep their tempers, and the people who act as if they were always under a burden of trouble and feeling sorry for themselves. You can't make that sort of a person

over; you can't do anything with them profitably, but get rid of him.

The man built a great business. That ethic created a great America. Today, he would be in big trouble, just like the hotel business, just like the economy.

Rothbard did not hesitate to strike at the greatest of all sacred cows: the *Brown* decision:

> The fundamental basis of the Brown decision was rotten law because it was not law at all, but the supposed "science" of sociology. The crucial grounding of Brown was the alleged finding of the revered socialist Dr. Kenneth Clark that black schools in the South were not really equal to white because black students in segregated schools don't do as well as blacks in integrated schools. That was the basis, and from that came all the horrors of compulsory integration, forced busing, and white depopulation and decay of the inner cities. And what has been the result? It is universally acknowledged that the education of black students in current integrated schools is much worse than what they received in the segregated schools; and indeed, the old segregated black schools are now being looked upon as a veritable Golden Age. Indeed, the latest trend among blacks is to try to reestablish all-black grade schools and high schools. Very well, but from that, several things must follow. One is that since the sociology of the Brown decision is all wet, and Brown was based upon lousy sociology, that Brown should be reversed. It has also been ruefully

acknowledged by integrationists that black and white students always tend to segregate themselves voluntarily — socialize among themselves, eat by themselves in the school cafeteria, etc. Much as Jacobin integrationists deplore this phenomenon and try to discourage it, we have to recognize that the process is voluntary and natural, and that there is nothing wrong with it.

Are we "racists" for holding these views? This of course raises the question: what exactly is "racism"? I want to look at two words that the State and its hangers-on have employed with much success on behalf of increases in government power. One is racism. The other is equality.

What exactly is "racism"? We almost never hear a definition. I doubt anyone really knows what it is. If you're inclined to dispute this, ask yourself why, if racism truly is something clear and determinate, there is such ceaseless disagreement over which thoughts and behaviors are "racist" and which are not?

If put on the spot, the average person would probably define racism along the lines of how Murray N. Rothbard defined anti-Semitism, involving hatred and/or the intention to carry out violence, whether State-directed or otherwise, against the despised group:

It seems to me that there are only two supportable and defensible definitions of anti-Semitism: one, focusing on the subjective mental state of the person, and the other "objectively," on the actions he undertakes or the policies he advocates. For the first, the

> best definition of anti-Semitism is simple and
> conclusive: a person who hates all Jews....

How, unless we are someone's close friend, or shrink, can we know what lies in a person's heart? Perhaps then the focus should be, not on the subject's state of heart or mind, but on a proposition that can be checked by observers who don't know the man personally. In that case, we should focus on the objective rather than the subjective, that is the person's actions or advocacies. Well, in that case, the only rational definition of an anti-Semite is one who advocates political, legal, economic, or social disabilities to be levied against Jews (or, of course, has participated in imposing them).

This, then, seems reasonable: (1) someone is a racist if he hates a particular racial group, but (2) since we can't read people's minds, and since accusing people of hating an entire group of people is a fairly serious charge, instead of vainly trying to read the suspect's mind we ought instead to see if he favors special disabilities against the group in question.

Back to Rothbard:

> But am I not redefining anti-Semitism out
> of existence? Certainly not. On the subjec-
> tive definition, by the very nature of the sit-
> uation, I don't know any such people, and I
> doubt whether the Smear Bund does either.
> On the objective definition, where outsiders
> can have greater knowledge, and setting aside
> clear-cut anti-Semites of the past, there are
> in modern America authentic anti-Semites:
> groups such as the Christian Identity move-
> ment, or the Aryan Resistance, or the author
> of the novel *Turner's Diaries*. But these are

marginal groups, you say, of no account and not worth worrying about? Yes, fella, and that is precisely the point.

On the other hand, maybe a "racist" is someone who believes different groups tend to have common characteristics, even while acknowledging the axiomatic point that each individual person is unique. But whether it's family structure, a penchant for alcoholism, a reputation for hard work, or a great many other qualities, Thomas Sowell has assembled a vast body of work showing that these traits are not even close to being distributed equally across populations.

The Chinese, for example, gained reputations in countries all over the world for working very hard, often under especially difficult conditions. (As a matter of fact, this is one of the reasons American labor unions despised Chinese workers in the nineteenth century.) By the mid-twentieth century, the Chinese minority dominated major sectors of the Malaysian economy even though they were officially discriminated against in the Malaysian constitution, and earned twice the income of the average Malay. They owned the vast majority of the rice mills in Thailand and the Philippines. They conducted more than 70 percent of the retail trade in Thailand, Indonesia, Cambodia, the Philippines, and Malaysia.

We could tell a similar story about Armenians in various parts of the world, as well as Jews and East Indians. Japanese-Americans went from being so badly discriminated against that they were confined to camps during World War II to equaling whites in income by 1959 and exceeding whites in income a decade later by one-third.

Likewise for Germans, whose reputations and accomplishments in craftsmanship, science, and technology have been evident not only in Germany but also among Germans in the US, Brazil, Australia, Czechoslovakia, and Chile. They had more prosperous farms than Irish farmers in eighteenth-century Ireland, than Brazilian farmers in Brazil, Russian farmers in Russia, and Chilean farmers in Chile.

Jews earn higher incomes than Hispanics in the US; this, we are solemnly told, is the result of "discrimination." Oh, really? As Sowell points out, how then are we to explain why Jews earn higher incomes than Hispanics *in Hispanic countries*?

According to the inane rules governing American society, Sowell, being black himself, is permitted to discuss such phenomena, while the rest of us face demonization, destroyed careers, and ruined reputations should we make note of any of this forbidden testimony.

In order not to be suspected of "racism," therefore, one must play it as safe as possible by at least pretending to believe the following propositions:

• income disparities among groups are explainable entirely or in very large part by "discrimination";

• if a minority group is "underrepresented" in a particular profession, the cause must be "racism";

• if minority students are disproportionately disciplined in school, the cause must be "racism," even when the teachers involved themselves belong to the same minority group;

• if test scores — both in school and in the private sector — differ by racial group, this is evidence that the tests are culturally biased, even though the questions showing the greatest disparity happen to have the least cultural content.

Not one of these statements is defensible, needless to say, but every one of them must be believed. Skeptics are, of course, "racist."

The following opinions or propositions have all been declared "racist" at one point or another, by one source or another:

- affirmative action is undesirable;
- antidiscrimination law is a violation of private property rights and freedom of contract;
- *Brown v. Board of Education* was based on faulty reasoning;
- the extent of racism in American society is exaggerated.

There are many grounds on which one could advance these claims. But since according to popular left-wing sites like Daily Kos, ThinkProgress, and Media Matters it is "racist" to believe in any of them, it doesn't matter what your arguments are. You are a "racist." Protest all you like, but the more you try, the more the commissars smear and ridicule you. You may pretend that you have logically sound and morally unimpeachable reasons for your views, but this is all a smokescreen for "racism" as far as the commissars are concerned. *The only way you can satisfy them now is by abandoning your views* (and even then they'll still question your sincerity), even though you do not hold them on disreputable grounds.

Thus charges of "racism" nearly always involve attempted mind reading — e.g., *that person claims to oppose antidiscrimination law out of some kind of principle, but we know it's because he's a racist.*

To see libertarians, who of course should know better, jumping on the thought-control bandwagon, or pretending that the whole issue is about the freedom to be a jerk, is extremely short-sighted and most unfortunate. The State uses the "racism" racket as justification for its further extension of power over education, employment, wealth redistribution, and a good deal else. Meanwhile, it silences critics of State violence with its magic, never-defined word "racism," an accusation the critic has to spend the rest of his life trying to disprove, only to discover that the race hustlers will not lift the curse until he utterly abases himself and repudiates his entire philosophy.

If he tries to defend himself by protesting that he has close friends who belong to the group he is accused of hating, he'll be ridiculed more than ever. Here's Rothbard again:

> I also want to embellish a point: All my life, I have heard anti-anti-Semites sneer at Gentiles who, defending themselves against the charge of anti-Semitism, protest that "some of my best friends are Jews." This phrase is always sneered at, as if easy ridicule is a refutation of the argument. But it seems to me that ridicule is habitually used here, precisely because the argument is conclusive. If some of Mr. X's best friends are indeed Jews, it is absurd and self-contradictory to claim that he is anti-Semitic. And that should be that.

It's hard to argue with Rothbard here. If someone had been accused of disliking ground beef, but it could be shown that he very much enjoyed hamburgers and goulash, that would pretty much demolish the accusation, wouldn't it?

I know no one who hates entire groups, and those people who do are in such a tiny minority that their organizations are equal parts lunatic and FBI informant. Likewise, I know no one who favors the use of official violence against particular groups.

We should want to treat people justly and with respect, of course. Any decent person feels that way. But how and why does "equality" enter the picture, except in the trivial and obvious libertarian sense that we should all equally refrain from aggression against one another?

The State likes nothing more than to declare war on drugs, or terrorism, or poverty, or "inequality." The State loves "equality" as an organizing principle, because it can never be achieved. In the course of trying, the State acquires ever more power over ever more practices and institutions. Anyone who questions the premise of equality is hectored out of polite society. Quite a racket, this, and certainly no place for libertarians to be.

If it's material equality we want, it would vanish the moment after we achieved it, as soon as people resumed their normal spending patterns and the goods and services offered by some people were more highly valued than those offered by others. If it's "equality of opportunity," then we would have to abolish the family, as so many socialist schemes have seriously contemplated, since conditions in the household play such an important role in children's success.

Yes, of course we oppose the inequality that results from special State privilege enjoyed by certain people and groups. But the real issue there isn't inequality per se, but justice and private property.

Even the old saw about equality in the eyes of God isn't quite right. Erik von Kuehnelt-Leddihn, the traditional Catholic and classical liberal, noted that Judas, who betrayed Christ, was in no way the "equal" of the beloved disciple, and that the origins of "equality" lay in Lucifer's urge to be the equal of Christ. He added:

> Egalitarianism under the best circumstances becomes hypocrisy; if sincerely accepted and believed in, its menace is greater. Then all actual inequalities appear without exception to be unjust, immoral, intolerable. Hatred, unhappiness, tension, a general maladjustment is the result. The situation is even worse when brutal efforts are made to *establish* equality through a process of artificial leveling ("social engineering") which can only be done by force, restrictions, or terror, and the outcome is a complete loss of liberty.

If we want to be free, therefore, we must shun the State, its methods, and its language.

These days, practically every conceivable group is quick to charge discrimination. Unfortunately, the old are no exception. Concerning the issue of age discrimination, the Supreme Court in *Meacham v. Knolls* said that the burden of proof resides on the employer. If a company lays off too many older people (meaning, incredibly, people older than 40), it is under the gun, and must show that factors other than age account for the disparate impact. Otherwise, the courts will rule in favor of the plaintiffs and the business will be forced to fork over, even to the point of bankruptcy.

The age-discrimination law in question is 40 years old and an embedded part of the machinery of social planning by the courts. This decision is yet another move toward government control, but the real problem is more fundamental. Step back and think what it means for the government to make and enforce such a law.

Labor relations are as complex as any human relations. There are many reasons why people choose to associate or not associate. How do you decide whom to invite to a birthday? What are the standards you use? There is a scarcity of space and food, so you must discriminate in some way. There is no choice about that.

Think of the last party you held. There are some people you did not invite simply because you can't stand those people, usually for many reasons. And there are some who just might not mix well with others. Some people you want to invite but cannot because you have to cut the list somewhere.

Now imagine that the government appoints a party planner who says that you can invite or not invite whomever you want, provided that one consideration is not part of the mix: you must not decline to invite someone on grounds of hair color. Now, it may never have occurred to you to think along these lines. But now you have to. You notice that you have no redheads attending the party, much to your alarm.

What if this fact is taken as evidence that you are discriminating? Will it? You can't know for sure. You think again: even if no redheads are coming, this is surely not the reason why you are not inviting them. There are other factors, too many factors to name. In any case, how can the state's party planner know for sure what your motivations are? Isn't it astounding that a government agency would presume to read your mind, know your heart, and discern your innermost emotions and motives?

Truly it is totalitarian.

It is precisely the same in workplace management. There are an unending variety of factors that go into the makeup of the workforce of a single firm. How the mix turns out in the end is not something you can entirely plan. It might be dictated by any of a million factors depending on time and place.

The state says that you the employer may not discriminate on grounds of age. Fine, you think. You would never think to do that. You just want a job well done. But let's say your firm is heavily into new technologies. Everyone must have great programming skills and quickly adapt to new web interfaces and innovations.

That has no direct bearing on age. A 60-year-old can in principle be just right for the job. But it so happens that the young have more technological skills than the old. Your workforce, then, is dominated by people under 40. Then a Federal Reserve recession comes along, and you must choose the better programmers. The remaining people over 40 are cut.

Have you discriminated on grounds of age? Not to your mind. You are thinking only of job skills and profitability. But from the perspective of a government planner with an agenda, it is different. Looking at the facts, it seems like a clear case of age discrimination.

With this new court decision, the burden of proof is on you to show otherwise. But how can something like the absence of a motivation be demonstrated? Now, it is possible or even likely that you might be able to show that factors other than age constitute the main reason for the disparity. But it is a toss-up as to whether the court or the EEOC will agree with you.

The only way to be off the hook completely is to pad your workforce with people hired *because* they are older. In the name of proving that you are not discriminating against a group, your only protection is to discriminate in *favor* of that group. And by doing so, you are necessarily discriminating against other groups, since young people will be turned way to make room for the older group.

But isn't this a case of age discrimination of a "reverse" sort? Of course. After all, everyone is either young or old. The charge that the employer is weighing decisions by age can be trumped up in every case one can imagine. Here we see an amazing thicket, created entirely by a state that presumes the capacity and the right to read minds like a swami guru or mystic soothsayer. The state has assigned to itself superhuman powers, and it is up to you to obey.

In contrast, here is what the free market permits. Employers can hire or fire for any reason they want. Employers can be biased, bigoted, or have poor judgment, but it is the employers' judgment to make. The same is true of employees. They can quit for any reason, including one that discriminates against some trait of the employer.

Imagine if the state said that you may not quit your job on grounds that you dislike your boss's age, race, religion, or sex. If that is your reason, you must stay working there. We would all recognize that this is a case of involuntary servitude. It is an attack on freedom. So why do we not see that it is the same with the employer?

Under freedom, if an employer decides, for no good reason, that employees should not be older than 40, that is his judgment. If it is a bad decision, the competition will gain an edge by hiring the people who have been passed over.

A final point about the employee. Would you want to work for a company that doesn't really want you there, that is only maintaining your job for fear of the bureaucrat? That is not a prescription for a happy life. The happy life comes through permitting maximum freedom to associate and choose — a freedom that applies to everyone and under all circumstances, without exception.

And what about the disabled? In the 1930s, the great excuse for the dole was unemployment. In the 1960s, poverty. But in the victim-ridden twenty-first century, it is summed up in one word: disability, and what a preposterous word it is.

Disability: falling short of the average capacity for accomplishing a task, any task. Just as ability is a universal human trait, so too is disability. How many tenured professors in this country can play volleyball? How many Olympic athletes will someday be tenured professors? Everyone is disabled in some particular way.

The idea that a disability as such should mark a person as a victim stems from a nutty egalitarian assumption, namely, that all people should have exactly the same capacity for accomplishing any and all tasks. A Marxist or Leninist might conjure up such a fantasy, but it is utterly alien to normal human experience.

Yes, there are people who are, on the whole more disabled and there are those who are, on the whole, more able. But that does not prevent people from cooperating to their mutual advantage. The point of freedom and the division of labor is that people discover their own comparative advantages and skills and concentrate on them while avoiding areas where they are, comparatively, less skilled. Thanks to the free market, there is a place for everyone within this brilliant system.

Then in walks the state. The state says: no, your lack of ability in a particular area entitles you to the property of others. You have no value that the state does not grant you. Your status with the state entitles you to impose yourself on employers. It entitles you to live off the fat of the land and do no work, so long as you can muster enough pathos to convince an administrative judge of your plight.

This crazy system has a long history, but it has really taken off since the last President Bush made such a fuss about the Americans With Disabilities Act. That act is problem enough for American business, but the larger effect has been politico-cultural. It said to an entire generation of workers that if you can discover anything about you that is slightly discomforting, it might entitle you to an early retirement.

Do you find it discomforting to sit for six straight hours during an eight-hour day, or to stand for two straight hours? If you can possibly think of circumstances under which the answer is yes, you are probably eligible for a fat check from the government and all the medical benefits you can use.

Same goes for the great racket of our age: mental disability. Not that there is any doubt that plenty of people are afflicted with grave mental disabilities (look at the Executive Branch!). But bureaucracies are in no position to judge the scientific merit of each case, and so, inevitably, the entire issue becomes political. And if you doubt that mental disability is a disease over which the entire national wealth should be redistributed, you are a heartless troll.

In ten years, the amount transferred from your wallet to those living off disability claims has more than doubled, and become the largest income-support program in the federal budget ($60 billion), larger than unemployment benefits or food stamps.

Here's how it works. Let's say you are a low-skilled laborer who loses a job. You are sitting at home trying to figure out what to do. In the old days, the answer was: go out and get another job, even if it means lowering the price for your labor.

After the Great Society there was always the option of going on welfare. But these days, there are many strings attached to receiving welfare. The benefits are not fabulous, and bureaucrats bother you to do things like enroll in a job-training program.

After 1990, the word got around: disability is the most reliable cash cow. All you do is make a claim that is impossible to refute. The overwhelming numbers of disabilities claims come down to two essential sources: back trouble and mental disability. Who is to say you don't have back trouble? Actually, does anyone over the age of 40 *not* have some form of back trouble? As for mental disability, there's nothing like idle hands to create the illusion of grave mental trouble.

It's not quite an outright scam. Most of the lounge lizards are fully convinced that they have a problem that justifies getting a check. You can try this yourself. Next time you are at the mall, stand on a planter, wave five one-hundred dollar bills and say: if anyone has back trouble, this money is yours. If you had an unlimited pot of taxpayers' money, you could blow $60 billion in an afternoon.

No discussion of disability is complete without drawing attention to the role of lawyers. Whole law firms have been established and profited from shepherding disability claims through the courts. If Christ asked his disciples to be fishers of men, these law firms are fishers of victims, and they use your money as bait.

If the *New York Times* is right that disability is growing at alarming rates, and without end, the time could come when the whole of the American welfare state will be recast as an egalitarian disability assistance fund. And who is willing to stand up to this? Who is willing to tear away the mask of the disability movement and expose it as the proto-socialist plot that it is?

Let us draw some lessons. First, it is not enough to reform welfare. It must be abolished, lest the same programs be reinvented under a new rationale. Second, Republican welfare (the GOP gave the disability racket its biggest boost) is as bad or worse than any Democratic form. Third, the state's rob-and-pay machine is incredibly creative at using even the smallest wedge to accumulate massive power, in this case, using the working class to loot the middle class to fund the overclass.

On the first day of the Clarence Thomas hearings, Joe Biden waved a copy of *Takings* by University of Chicago law professor and economist Richard Epstein. In the work, Epstein argued that the welfare-regulatory state is unconstitutional. An apoplectic Biden demanded that Thomas repudiate *Takings*, which he quickly did.

If *Takings* drove Biden crazy, I can hardly wait to see him with a copy of Epstein's later book, *Forbidden*

Grounds, which advocates the repeal of all anti-discrimination laws, including the 1964 Civil Rights Act.

When that law was passed, we were promised a new dawn of happy race relations; 54 years later, bitterness between the races is the norm, especially in the workplace.

The only solution ever proposed is more government intervention. Are we really condemned to a series of evermore draconian and far-fetched civil rights bills? Yes, says Epstein, unless we deny the government the power to impose what is, in effect, racial central planning on the economy. Civil rights laws have made us poorer and angrier, while reducing efficiency, undermining merit, and expanding bureaucratic power. They must, he shows, be junked.

Wouldn't some people then discriminate? Sure, says Epstein, but so what? If a black beauty salon wants to exclude white hairdressers, that's fine. If an Asian restaurant wants a homogeneous workforce, that's fine too. Companies are more than abstract production units; they are micro-cultures. Shared tastes, values, and traditions can help a firm appeal to the Mexican market, for example. Why should it be forced to hire Anglos, especially since the free market ensures everyone a place in the division of labor?

But is this fair? Epstein says yes. Fairness means freedom to own property and to contract. Both require the repeal of the anti-discrimination laws.

Unless we do so, we will have gradual labor-market paralysis. Even the supposedly anti-quota 1964 Civil Rights Act effectively decreed them. When prosecutors found it difficult to prove bad motives by "non-diverse" firms, bureaucrats started playing Count the Minorities, and businessmen were forced to adopt quotas.

Ironically, this harmed the most vulnerable. To fill their quotas, employers seek only the most capable minorities. Others are shunned, no matter what the job category, since there is less chance they will work out, and firing any member of a federally protected minority — no matter how incompetent — can mean a federal lawsuit.

Epstein would also have us reevaluate the politicians who opposed the 1964 act; they correctly foresaw quotas and economy-wide social engineering. But even the most prescient did not predict the outlawing of written tests that fail to produce racially proportionate scores, or the banning of company rules against hiring ex-cons, since more blacks fall into that category than whites.

Moreover, Epstein shows that the damage is done by all anti-discrimination laws, whether based on race, age, sex, or disability. Therefore all of them must be wiped from the books.

Mandatory retirement, for example, is an essential part of the free market. You know, when hired, that at a certain age, you will have to retire. On the margin, employers want to have the option of hiring the younger employees who are more likely to be productive in years ahead. It does not always work out that way, of course, but such standards are more efficient than case-by-case determinations.

To retire an older person isn't to kick him out of the division of labor or to judge him incompetent. He can get other jobs in other capacities, if he wishes, and he is spared the humiliation of a competency hearing.

The government says that mandatory retirement ages discriminate against old people, as of course they do. Such a rule assumes that older people are different from younger ones, something the government refuses to recognize. The government claims there is no difference, but if that were true, private employers would not discriminate and there would be no issue.

What's next? Laws forbidding discrimination against the young? In fact, it's just the opposite, as the government refuses to allow anyone under 16 to work for a living.

The government's intervention in employment contracts is particularly egregious in universities. The Equal Employment Opportunity Commission is attempting to abolish mandatory retirement for tenured faculty. Amendments to the anti-age discrimination law in 1986 exempted universities until December 31, 1993, but the EEOC hasn't waited.

As Epstein notes, "The internal operation of universities (especially the prominent research universities) will suffer if mandatory retirement is eliminated — more I suspect, than most pessimists fear."

Given tenure, which tends to dampen productivity anyway, mandatory retirement is the only way to preserve the intellectual vitality of universities. Automatic tenure termination allows all parties to avoid endless evaluations by peers and administrators that could cause only bitter hatred. If the government forbids tenure termination, promising young scholars in economics and other disciplines will be crowded out.

So absurd are the EEOC's rules that if a university set up a panel to review the status of its oldest faculty, that itself would be a violation of anti-discrimination regulations.

The government forgets that many faculty whose tenure is terminated on schedule find teaching positions in other universities if they wish. A case in point is philosophy professor Paul Weiss, whose tenure at Yale ended in 1969. He left for Catholic University. Until the age of 91, the university kept him on a year-by-year contract. He required graduate students to help him get around and do his shopping and could not hear very well.

When the university sought to place Weiss on a part-time contract, he claimed age discrimination. Yes, but so what?

William F. Buckley, Jr., however, took the left-liberal view. This is just one more piece of evidence that, as Epstein says, all law against age discrimination ought to be "repealed forthwith." Like other anti-discrimination laws, they are an attack on property, the free market, and the freedom to contract. They serve special interests and state power, setting black against white, men against women, and young against old.

If this book isn't burned by the ACLU, it will permanently alter the debate on civil rights. For that, Epstein deserves the Pulitzer. But given today's climate, he may have to be satisfied with the spittle running down Biden's chin as he reads *Forbidden Grounds*. After all, a Biden denouncement can only increase sales.

Murray Rothbard has made clear the nature of the fanaticism that underlies the left's desire to impose its values on us and to destroy freedom in so doing:

> For some time I have been hammering at the theme that the main cultural and political

problem of our time is not "secular humanism." The problem with making secularism the central focus of opposition is that, by itself, secularism would totally lack the fanaticism, the demonic energy, the continuing and permanent drive to take over and remake the culture and the society, that has marked the left for two centuries. Logically, one would expect a secular humanist to be a passive skeptic, ready to adapt to almost any existing state of affairs; David Hume, for example, a philosophic disaster but quietly benign in social and political matters, would seem to be typical. Hardly a political and cultural menace.

No: the hallmark and the fanatical drive of the left for these past centuries has been in devoting tireless energy to bringing about, as rapidly as they can, their own egalitarian, collectivist version of a Kingdom of God on Earth. In short, this truly monstrous movement is what might be called "left-post-millennialist." It is messianic and post-millennialist because Man, not Christ or Providence, is supposed to bring about the Kingdom of God on Earth (KGE), that is, in the Christian version, that Christ is only supposed to return to earth after Man has established the 1,000-year KGE. It is leftist because in this version, the KGE is egalitarian and collectivist, with private property stamped out, and the world being run by a cadre or vanguard of Saints.

During the 1820s, the Protestant churches in the Northern states of the U.S. were taken over by a wave of post-millennial fanatics determined to impose on local, state, and federal governments, and even throughout the world, their own version of a theocratic statist KGE. A "Yankee" ethnocultural group had originated in New England, and had migrated to settle the northern areas of New York and the Middle-Western states. The Yankees were driven by the fanatical conviction that they themselves could not achieve salvation unless they did their best to maximize everyone else's: which meant, among other features, to devote their energies to instituting the sinless society of the KGE.

These newly mainstream Yankee Protestant churches were always statist, but the major emphasis in the early decades was the stamping out of "sin," sin being broadly defined as virtually any form of enjoyment. By the later years of the nineteenth century, however, economic collectivism received increasing attention by these left millennialist Protestants, and strictly theological and Christological concerns gradually faded away, culminating in the explicitly socialistic Social Gospel movement in all the Protestant churches. While every one of the Yankee Protestant denominations was infected and dominated by left millennialism, this heresy prevailed almost totally in the Methodist Church.

Academia has undergone a remarkable transformation in recent years. Take a look at the catalog of Duke University Press, once a prestigious publishing house. Today it features third-rate, race-obsessed, sex-obsessed, solipsistic tirades masquerading as scholarship.

Let's take a peek. In *Between Jesus and the Market: The Emotions That Matter in Right-Wing America*, Linda Kintz puzzles as to why "so many women are attracted to" conservative Christianity since it is "an antiwoman philosophy." And she criticizes the left for "underestimating the power" of public menaces like militias, Rush Limbaugh, and groups that promote "Christian entrepreneurship."

As revealing as Kintz's treatise must be, it is surpassed by Jane Lazarre's *Beyond the Whiteness of Whiteness*. This is her "memoir of coming to terms with" the reality that, though her father is black, her mother is Jewish, and her husband is black, she is not black but white, or so her biracial son reveals to her. This "painful truth" informs her "powerful meditation on motherhood and racism in America."

She's got a comrade in Katya Gibel Azoulay, who has written another classic, *Black, Jewish, and Interracial: It's Not the Color of Your Skin, But the Race of Your Kin, and Other Myths of Identity*. This worked is praised as a "brilliant analysis" by Michael Eric Dyson, author of *Between God and Gangsta Rap*. Think of both as companion volumes to *Displacing Whiteness*, edited by Ruth Frankenberg, which in turn is praised as "excellent" by David Roediger, author of *Towards the Abolition of Whiteness*.

Then there's the emerging classic *Novel Gazing: Queer Readings in Fiction* edited by Eve Kosofsky Sedgwick. The contributors "explore queer worlds of taste, texture, joy and ennui, focusing on such subjects as flogging, wizardry, exorcism, dance, Zionist desire, and Internet sexuality." At 520 pages, the publisher suggests it is "essential for all literary critics."

Indeed it may be, which is all we need to know about literary criticism, and the modern academy. It is possible, these days, for a student to blast through undergraduate and graduate school without being required to know the first thing about American and European history, constitutional law, Western literature, economics, or political philosophy.

Thanks to the proliferation of elective-based academic ghettos within the university, students can isolate themselves into a host of phony fields. And the message in each is one of malice: hate bourgeois civilization and the ideas and literature that spawned it. Spin that thought out, and you'll get an "A" most of the time. Ironically, the more prestigious the school, the more malevolent the teaching.

How can we account for the crumbling of the liberal arts education? It is not, as many conservative critics suggest, due to a mysterious evaporation of the canonical texts. Such a problem might be easily dealt with by gimmicks like "national standards." The problem has deeper roots in three institutional shifts that afflicted the academy from the New Deal to the present: democratization (1930–1960), affirmative action (1964–1985), and polylogism (1987–present).

It was a staple of American economic life, from the founding until quite recently, that each generation would be better off than the previous one. The level of education each generation could achieve was a reflection of the growing prosperity that capitalism made possible. But in time, cause and effect were reversed: instead of seeing how prosperity generated a better-educated public, it was widely believed that education by itself created prosperity.

The education myth took hold as the Great Depression hit, as parents aspired to put their children through college as a way out of lower-class living standards. On the face of it, this was an absurd assumption. Education is among the most economically costly activities a person can undertake. The student leaves the workforce during what would otherwise be some of his most productive years. He graduates with ratified knowledge which may or may not help him. Only some can benefit.

That's why, from ancient Greece until the twentieth century, higher education was reserved for the wealthiest and smartest segments of the population. Capitalism made the wealthy segment much larger, but it did not erase and could not erase distinctions between social and intellectual classes. Even in the freest societies, there has always existed a marked separation between an educated class and a working class, a separation that only violent intervention in the market could destroy.

And destroy it, it did. Academic standards began to unravel as early as the mid-1930s, with the growth of centralized, tax-funded higher education, and the democratization of elite private institutions. Cultural critic Albert Jay Nock saw this early on. He wrote in the *Atlantic Monthly*, much to the shock of readers, that academic standards would continue on their downward path so long as we embrace the idea that everyone is equally educable. The curriculum would be watered down to shore up that mythology.

Democratization received a huge boost after the Second World War, as the G.I. bill poured government aid into universities in unprecedented amounts. The purpose was not, as is assumed, to give soldiers academic training for civilian life. Government planners had wrongly feared the consequences of so many new entrants into the workforce. The purpose of the G.I. bill was to keep as many as possible out of the workforce, thereby restraining unemployment. In fact, a growing and recently unshackled economy was able to absorb all of them almost overnight. However, government control followed government money, as it always does, and one G.I. bill legacy was the virtual nationalization of accreditation boards and thus the centralization of educational standards. By the time of the civil-rights revolution of the early 1960s, universities would become instruments of federal race policy and its affirmative-action subtext. Quotas in admissions followed, and over the next decades, what was left of academia's high standards was pushed aside to accomplish egalitarian goals.

It was only a matter of time before egalitarian standards invaded the composition of the faculty itself. Special interest groups argued that it is as unjust to have predominantly white faculties as it is to have predominantly white student bodies, whether merit was involved or not.

The imposition of multiculturalism — where affirmative action professors guide affirmative-action students to degrees in the glories of affirmative action — was merely the mopping-up operation. Of course, the publishers joined forces to produce specialized books for these classes. One result is the Duke book catalog, not atypical for an academic press these days.

The key to understanding multiculturalism is Mises's 1957 classic *Theory and History*. He identified a central assumption of Marxist social theory: polylogism, the view that standards of reason are not independent of person and place.

Remarkably, as early as 1949, Mises, writing in *Human Action*, had seen how the left would apply this menacing doctrine to race theory. Racial polylogists nod in agreement with the Nazis who said there was a specifically "German" way of thinking that is valid in its own terms. The members of racial groups, too, have different structures of mind, and so all judgments regarding valid and invalid forms of reasoning are either arbitrary or an expression of group self-interest.

In practice, this results in the exaltation of irrationalism and the demand that any theory that asserts the universality of logic and truth — meaning practically all Western thought — is to be done away with. In modern academia, where polylogism reached its wits' end, there is only one invalid and even evil way of looking at the world: with Western eyes using Western concepts such as truth and reason.

Decent faculty and students have been subject to a terror campaign on behalf of this new and perverse orthodoxy. Faculty conduct their classes as best they can while avoiding conflicts and lawsuits; and students suffer through periodic Pol-Pot style re-education camps in the aftermath of any political flare-up.

Meanwhile, non-leftist faculty have been forced to drain serious, systematic thought from their presentations, for fear of the polylogist thought police. And students have been forced to suffer in silence as their dream of true learning turned into a politically correct nightmare.

In the social sciences, economics remains one of the few disciplines that has not been seriously damaged by the new polylogism. The profession has its share of feminist economists, who claim there is a specific woman's way of theorizing, but it has remained largely untouched by this nonsense. It has its own problems — positivism, unreal modeling techniques, and the planning mentality — but the student who likes economics is mostly spared the polylogism of the modern academy.

Indeed, just as it is possible for students to take only PC courses and read only Duke-style books, it is also possible for the conscientious student to avoid them. This is what the good student must do, or risk wasting years of his life.

Moreover, for a complete education, it is not enough to take classes only in fields that have yet to be bowdlerized. Wilhelm Röpke once commented that an economist who knows only economics can never be a good economist. To be thoroughly understood and intelligently applied, economics needs disciplines like history, philosophy, and the history of ideas. In short, economists need a liberal arts education of the sort that Mises, Rothbard, Menger, and Böhm-Bawerk had.

But where are they going to get it today? Every summer the Mises Institute holds an intensive program that attempts, in a small way, to make up for the deficiencies of modern education. The students who come our way are interested in economics in part because it *has* been spared the multicultural mania. And though they are among the brightest students in school today, they too have been denied an opportunity to root economics in a wider and more systematic worldview.

Our faculty provide this, and we see our summer university's value appreciating each year. This is expressed in the student evaluation forms, which praise the faculty's fearless approach above all else. These students typically continue on in their studies and obtain the requisite credentials for entering academic life themselves, all the while carrying on separate reading programs to give them the grounding in serious thought that the modern academy has denied them.

Contrary to the pessimism of many conservatives, there is no reason to despair. Our programs are reinforced by dissident faculty and curricula in independent-minded colleges and universities across the country. This dissident force, and their students, is growing larger by the day, and it displays a warrior-like courage.

The signs of success are all around us. The best students no longer believe the nonsense they are force-fed. A new generation is being raised up amid the excesses of egalitarianism, determined to reverse them.

In the long run, ideas can't rule by intimidation alone. When a new generation of brave and well-educated teachers has the lion's share of intellectual passion on its side, their opponents can be toppled.

CHAPTER 3

Immigration

WHETHER WE'RE TALKING ABOUT ILLEGAL immigration from Mexico and Central America, or birthright citizenship, or the migrants coming from the Middle East and Africa, the subject of immigration has been in the news and widely discussed. It is an issue fraught with potentially perilous consequences, so it is especially important for libertarians to understand it correctly.

I should note at the outset that in searching for the correct answer to this vexing problem I do not seek to claim originality. To the contrary, I draw much of what follows from two of the people whose work is indispensable to a proper understanding of the free society: Murray N. Rothbard and Hans-Hermann Hoppe.

Some libertarians have assumed that the correct libertarian position on immigration must be "open borders," or the completely unrestricted movement of people. Superficially, this appears correct: surely we believe in letting people go wherever they like!

But hold on a minute. Think about "freedom of speech," another principle people associate with libertarians. Do we really believe in freedom of speech as an abstract principle? That would mean I have the right to yell all during a movie, or the right to disrupt a Church service, or the right to enter your home and shout obscenities at you.

What we believe in are private property rights. No one has "freedom of speech" on my property, since I set the rules, and in the last resort I can expel someone. He can say whatever he likes on his own property, and on the property of anyone who cares to listen to him, but not on mine.

The same principle holds for freedom of movement. Libertarians do not believe in any such principle in the abstract. I do not have the right to wander into your house, or into your gated community, or into Disneyworld, or onto your private beach, or onto Jay-Z's private island. As with "freedom of speech," private property is the relevant factor here. I can move onto any property I myself own or whose owner wishes to have me. I cannot simply go wherever I like.

Now if all the parcels of land in the whole world were privately owned, the solution to the so-called immigration problem would be evident. In fact, it might be more accurate to say that there would be no immigration problem in the first place. Everyone moving somewhere new would have to have the consent of the owner of that place.

When the state and its so-called public property enter the picture, though, things become murky, and it takes extra effort to uncover the proper libertarian position.

Shortly before his death, Murray Rothbard published an article called "Nations by Consent: Decomposing the Nation State." He had begun rethinking the assumption that libertarianism committed us to open borders.

He noted, for instance, the large number of ethnic Russians whom Stalin settled in Estonia. This was not done so that Baltic people could enjoy the fruits of diversity. It never is. It was done in an attempt to destroy an existing culture, and in the process to make a people more docile and less likely to cause problems for the Soviet empire.

Murray wondered: does libertarianism require me to support this, much less to celebrate it? Or might there be more to the immigration question after all?

And here Murray posed the problem just as I have: in a fully private-property society, people would have to be invited onto whatever property they traveled through or settled on.

If every piece of land in a country were owned by some person, group, or corporation, this would mean that no person could enter unless invited to enter and allowed to rent or purchase property. A totally privatized country would be as closed as the particular property owners desire. It seems clear, then, that the regime of open borders that exists *de facto* in the US and Western Europe really amounts to a compulsory opening by the central state, the state in charge of all streets and public land areas, and does not genuinely reflect the wishes of the proprietors.

In the current situation, on the other hand, immigrants have access to public roads, public transportation, public buildings, and so on. Combine this with the state's other curtailments of private property rights, and the result is artificial demographic shifts that would not occur in a free market. Property owners are forced to associate and do business with individuals they might otherwise avoid.

"Commercial property owners such as stores, hotels, and restaurants are no longer free to exclude or restrict access as they see fit," writes Hans Hoppe.

> Employers can no longer hire or fire who they wish. In the housing market, landlords are no longer free to exclude unwanted tenants. Furthermore, restrictive covenants are compelled to accept members and actions in violation of their very own rules and regulations.

Hans continues:

> By admitting someone onto its territory, the state also permits this person to proceed on public roads and lands to every domestic resident's doorsteps, to make use of all public facilities and services (such as hospitals and schools), and to access every commercial establishment, employment, and residential housing, protected by a multitude of nondiscrimination laws.

It is rather unfashionable to express concern for the rights of property owners, but whether the principle is popular or not, a transaction between two people should not occur unless both of those people want it to. This is the very core of libertarian principle.

In order to make sense of all this and reach the appropriate libertarian conclusion, we have to look more closely at what public property really is and who, if anyone, can be said to be its true owner. Hans has devoted some of his own work to precisely this question. There are two positions we must reject: that public property is owned by the government, or that public property is unowned, and is therefore comparable to land in the state of nature, before individual property titles to particular parcels of land have been established.

Certainly we cannot say public property is owned by the government, since government may not legitimately own anything. Government acquires its property by force, usually via the intermediary of taxation. A libertarian cannot accept that kind of property acquisition as morally legitimate, since it involves the initiation of force (the extraction of tax dollars) on innocent people. Hence government's pretended property titles are illegitimate.

But neither can we say that public property is *unowned*. Property in the possession of a thief is not unowned, even if at the moment it does not happen to be held by the rightful owner. The same goes for so-called public property. It was purchased and developed by means of money seized from the taxpayers. They are the true owners.

(This, incidentally, was the correct way to approach de-socialization in the former communist regimes of Eastern Europe. All those industries were the property of the people who had been looted to build them, and those people should have received shares in proportion to their contribution, to the extent it could have been determined.)

In an anarcho-capitalist world, with all property privately owned, "immigration" would be up to each individual property owner to decide. Right now, on the other hand, immigration decisions are made by a central authority, with the wishes of property owners completely disregarded. The correct way to proceed, therefore, is to decentralize decision-making on immigration to the lowest possible level, so that we approach ever more closely the proper libertarian position, in which individual property owners consent to the various movements of peoples.

Ralph Raico, our great libertarian historian, once wrote:

> Free immigration would appear to be in a different category from other policy decisions, in that its consequences permanently and radically alter the very composition of the democratic political body that makes those decisions. In fact, the liberal order, where and to the degree that it exists, is the product of a highly complex cultural development. One wonders, for instance, what would become of the liberal society of Switzerland under a regime of "open borders."

Switzerland is in fact an interesting example. Before the European Union got involved, the immigration policy of Switzerland approached the kind of system we are describing here. In Switzerland, localities decided on immigration, and immigrants or their employers had to pay to admit a prospective migrant. In this way, residents could better ensure that their communities would be populated by people who would add value and who would not stick them with the bill for a laundry list of "benefits."

Obviously, in a pure open borders system, the Western welfare states would simply be overrun by foreigners seeking tax dollars. As libertarians, we should of course celebrate the demise of the welfare state. But to expect a sudden devotion to *laissez-faire* to be the likely outcome of a collapse in the welfare state is to indulge in naïveté of an especially preposterous kind.

Can we conclude that an immigrant should be considered "invited" by the mere fact that he has been hired by an employer? No, says Hans, because the employer does not assume the full cost associated with his new employee. The employer partially externalizes the costs of that employee on the taxpaying public:

> Equipped with a work permit, the immigrant is allowed to make free use of every public facility: roads, parks, hospitals, schools, and no landlord, businessman, or private associate is permitted to discriminate against him as regards housing, employment, accommodation, and association. That is, the immigrant comes invited with a substantial fringe benefits package paid for not (or only partially) by the immigrant employer (who allegedly has extended the invitation), but by other domestic proprietors as taxpayers who had no say in the invitation whatsoever.

These migrations, in short, are not market outcomes. They would not occur on a free market. What we are witnessing are examples of subsidized movement. Libertarians defending these mass migrations as if they were market phenomena are only helping to discredit and undermine the true free market.

Moreover, as Hans points out, the "free immigration" position is not analogous to free trade, as some libertarians have erroneously claimed. In the case of goods being traded from one place to another, there is always and necessarily a willing recipient. The same is not true for "free immigration."

To be sure, it is fashionable in the US to laugh at words of caution about mass immigration. Why, people made predictions about previous waves of immigration, we're told, and we all know those didn't come true. Now for one thing, those waves were all followed by swift and substantial immigration reductions, during which time society adapted to these pre-welfare state population movements. There is virtually no prospect of any such reductions today. For another, it is a fallacy to claim that because some people incorrectly predicted a particular outcome at a particular time, therefore that outcome is impossible, and anyone issuing words of caution about it is a contemptible fool.

The fact is, politically enforced multiculturalism has an exceptionally poor track record. The twentieth century afforded failure after predictable failure. Whether it's Czechoslovakia, Yugoslavia, the Soviet Union, or Pakistan and Bangladesh, or Malaysia and Singapore, or the countless places with ethnic and religious divides that have not yet been resolved to this day, the evidence suggests something rather different from the tale of universal brotherhood that is such a staple of leftist folklore.

No doubt some of the new arrivals will be perfectly decent people, despite the US government's lack of interest in encouraging immigration among the skilled and capable. But some will not. The three great crime waves in US history — which began in 1850, 1900, and 1960 — coincided with periods of mass immigration.

Crime isn't the only reason people may legitimately wish to resist mass immigration. If four million Americans showed up in Singapore, that country's culture and society would be changed forever. And no, it is not true that libertarianism would in that case require the people of Singapore to shrug their shoulders and say it was nice having our society while it lasted but all good things must come to an end. No one in Singapore would want that outcome, and in a free society, they would actively prevent it.

In other words, it's bad enough we have to be looted, spied on, and kicked around by the state. Should we also have to pay for the privilege of cultural destructionism, an outcome the vast majority of the state's taxpaying subjects do not want and would actively prevent if they lived in a free society and were allowed to do so?

The very cultures that the incoming migrants are said to enrich us with could not have developed had they been constantly bombarded with waves of immigration by peoples of radically different cultures. So the multicultural argument doesn't even make sense.

It is impossible to believe that the US or Europe will be a freer place after several more decades of uninterrupted mass immigration. Given the immigration patterns that the US and EU governments encourage, the long-term result will be to make the constituencies for continued government growth so large as to be practically unstoppable. Open-borders libertarians active at that time will scratch their heads and claim not to understand why their promotion of free markets is having so little success. Everybody else will know the answer.

Of course, as Rothbard noted, the best possible solution to the immigration problem is total privatization:

> Under total privatization, many local conflicts and "externality" problems — not merely the immigration problem — would be neatly settled. With every locale and neighborhood owned by private firms, corporations, or contractual communities, true diversity would reign, in accordance with the preferences of each community. Some neighborhoods would be ethnically or economically diverse, while others would be ethnically or economically homogeneous. Some localities would permit pornography or prostitution or drugs or abortions, others would prohibit any or all of them. The prohibitions would not be state imposed, but would simply be requirements for residence or use of some person's or community's land area. While statists who have the itch to impose their values on everyone else would be disappointed, every group or interest would at least have the satisfaction of living in neighborhoods of people who share its values and preferences. While neighborhood ownership would not provide Utopia or a panacea for all conflicts, it would at least provide a [second-best] solution that most people might be willing to live with.

CHAPTER **4**

Environmentalism

I am a sinner but unrepentant. You see, I don't practice environmentalism, and I don't believe in it. I don't recycle and I don't conserve — except when it pays to do so. I like clean air — really clean air, like the kind an air conditioner makes. I like the bug-free indoors. I like development, as in buildings, concrete, capitalism, prosperity. I don't like swamps (and that goes for any "wetland," even the ballyhooed "Everglades") or jungles ("rainforests"). I see all animals except dogs and cats as likely disease carriers, unless they're in a zoo.

When PBS runs a special on animal intelligence, I am unmoved. I'm glad for the dolphins that they can squeak. I'm happy for the ape that he can sign for his food. How charming for the bees that they organize themselves so well for work. But that doesn't give them rights over me. Their only real value comes from what they can do for man.

According to modern political and religious doctrine, all these views make me a sinner. The mainline churches long ago became quasi-Manichaean, heralding blessed poverty and swearing never to disturb blessed nature with the stain of human action. And we all know about the vogue of New Age religions. Public-school kids are taught the religion of eco-sentimentalism.

Even the new Catholic Catechism seems mushy on the subject. "Man's dominion over inanimate and other living beings granted by the Creator is not absolute ... it requires a religious respect for the integrity of creation" (par. 2416). I have no idea what this means. It seems like a sop to the new paganism. Do killer bees and killer bacteria have "integrity" worthy of "religious respect"? To my mind, nature is only valuable if it serves man's needs. If it does not, it must be transformed.

Even in free-market circles, I'm expected to herald the beauty and moral integrity of nature before I discuss property rights and markets. In fact, "free-market environmentalists" insist that we accept the goals of the greens, while only rejecting some of their statist means as the best way to achieve those goals. I don't buy it. The environmentalists are targeting everything I love, and the struggle between us and them is fundamental.

Only the Randians can be counted on to make any sense on this issue. They assert what used to be the Christian position only a few decades ago: namely, that man occupies the highest spot in the great chain of being. The interests of no animal, no species, no living thing, should be permitted to trump the need for human flourishing. But for such outrageous talk, the Randians have been banished by many libertarians on grounds that their strategy is all wrong.

One wise Randian once implored me to closely examine the word "environment." What does it refer to, he asked? Well, you can tick through the list of environmental concerns: air, water, animals, trees, the ozone, etc. But where does it stop? What are the boundaries of what is called the environment? What it really means, he said, is: "anything but man." He was right. A perfect environment would be a world without people. How monstrous to allow the greens to take even one step toward this goal!

Not just Rand, but also St. Augustine believed that the purpose of nature is to serve man:

> Some attempt to extend this command ["Thou Shalt Not Kill"] even to beasts and cattle, as if it forbade us to take life from any creature. But if so, why not extend it also to the plants, and all that is rooted in and nourished by the earth? For though this class of creatures have no sensation, yet they also are said to live, and consequently they can die; and therefore, if violence be done them, can be killed. So, too, the apostle, when speaking of the seeds of such things as these, says, "That which thou sowest is not quickened except it die;" and in the Psalm it is said, "He killed their vines with hail." Must we therefore reckon it a breaking of this commandment, "Thou shalt not kill," to pull a flower? Are we thus insanely to countenance the foolish error of the Manichaeans? Putting aside, then, these ravings, if, when we say, Thou shalt not kill, we do not understand this of the plants, since they have no sensation, nor of the irrational

> animals that fly, swim, walk, or creep, since
> they are dissociated from us by their want of
> reason, and are therefore by the just appoint-
> ment of the Creator subjected to us to kill or
> keep alive for our own uses.

How glorious, St. Augustine also wrote, to see human habitations spreading where once unchecked nature reigned. That's my view too. I don't care how many homilies I hear about the glories of nature, from the pulpit or Congress or the media, I'm against it, unless it has been changed by man into something useful or otherwise valuable. Things that grow are for food, clothing, decoration, or lawns. All swamps should be drained. All rainforests turned over to productive agriculture.

Not being a do-it-myselfer, my favorite section of the hardware store features bug killers, weed killers, varmint traps, and poisons of all sorts. These killer potions represent high civilization and capitalism. The bags are decorated with menacing pictures of ants, roaches, tweezer-nosed bugs, and other undesirable things, to remind us that the purpose of these products is to snuff out bug life so it won't menace the only kind of life that has a soul and thus the only kind of life that matters: man.

The only problem with pesticides is that they aren't strong enough. "Fire-ant killer" only causes the little buggers to pick up and move. Why? Some time back, the government banned the best pesticide of all: DDT. As a result, the country is filled with menacing, disease-car-rying flying and crawling insects. Whole swaths of for-merly wonderful vacation property has been wrecked because we are not permitted to use the only substance that ever really worked to wipe these things out. In the third world, many thousands have died since the abolition of DDT thanks to increased malaria and other bug-borne diseases. All this because we have decided that bugs have a greater right to life than we do. All this because we ignore a key tenet of Western thought: all things not human are "subjected to us to kill or keep alive for our own uses."

Such thoughts can get you arrested these days because environmentalism is our official religion. Consider the Styrofoam question. I refuse to hold a paper cup with hot coffee, not when a perfectly wonderful insulated cup is available. When I demand the coffee shop give me Styrofoam, they shrink back like Dracula before the crucifix. I explain that Styrofoam takes up less than 0.001 percent of landfill space, and that inked paper is actually more poisonous for ground water, so maybe they better not subscribe to the *New York Times*, but it doesn't matter. For them, paper cups are holy and Styrofoam is the devil. Evidence just doesn't matter.

We know where environmentalism actually came from. The left once claimed that the state could make us better off. The bigger the government, the more prosperous we would be. When that turned out not to be true, they changed their tune. Suddenly, they began to condemn prosperity itself, and the place of the oppressed proletariat was taken by oppressed members of the animal, plant, and insect kingdoms. We have adopted poverty as a policy goal, complete with its own civic code of ethics.

From time immemorial until the day before yesterday, Western man has seen nature as the enemy, and rightly so. It is dangerous and deadly. For the sake of our own survival it must be tamed, cut, curbed, controlled. That is the first task of civilization. The first step to civilization's destruction is the failure to understand this, or to call this attitude a sin.

It might take a while to sink in, but the global warming cause is on the skids. Two issues are taking the whole project down: it is getting cooler not warmer (and hence the change of the rhetoric to a vague concern over "climate change"), and the email scandal of 2009 proved that this really is an opinion cartel with preset views not driven by science.

Oh sure, people are said that climategate is not really very serious and was only being exploited by Fox News and the like. And it's true that not all measures of global temperature show cooling and that the science can be complex.

On that basis, the *New York Times* urged us to ignore the outpouring. "It is also important not to let one set of purloined email messages undermine the science and the clear case for action, in Washington and in Copenhagen."

Yes, a clear case. Come on. The whole political agenda of these people is now being seriously questioned. It is no longer a slam-dunk case that we are going to have world central planning in order to control the climate and protect the holy earth from the effects of industrialization. Oh, and tax us good and hard in the process.

But you know what is most tragic to me about this? This whole hysteria led to a fantastic diversion of energy on the left side of the political spectrum. Instead of working against war and the police state, issues on which the left tends to be pretty good, instincts were diverted to the preposterous cause of creating a statist system for global thermometer management.

The effort to whip everyone up into a frenzy over this began over 20 ten years ago. Every lefty fundraising letter harped on the issue, and demanded people commit their lives to it, explaining that if mother earth dies, then all is lost. It is a more important issue than all the rest, the litmus test to determine whether you are a friend or an enemy.

This made it very difficult for libertarians to cooperate with the left. Sure, there are some libertarian ideas for dealing with pollution, but none as compelling as central planning, and there was never any way that we would go along with that idea. The costs associated with dismantling industrial civilization outweigh even the worst-case global-warming scenario.

And methodologically, the whole thing was always nuts. If we can't determine cause and effect now with certainty, how in the heck will we be able to determine it after the world state controls our carbon emissions, and impoverishes us in the process? No one will ever be in a position to say whether the policy worked or failed. That is not a good basis for enacting legislation.

Meanwhile, the left threw everything it had into this hysteria. Protests, letters, billions in spending, frenzy, moral passion, mania, witch hunts — you name it. You would swear that climate change was the issue of the millennium for these people.

Meanwhile, the police state has made unbelievable advances. We all live today in fear of the state's "security" apparatus. Airports have become living chapters in a dystopian novel. The local police treat us like potential terrorists. Crossing the US border is becoming reminiscent of East Germany. You can't go anywhere without your papers.

And where has the left been while the whole world is being Nazified? Worrying about my barbecue grill out back.

Then there is the war issue. The scary George Bush started war after war and kept them going to bolster his own power and prestige, creating as many enemies as possible through provocations and making up enemies if he had to. He funded a bubble that wrecked the economy and destroyed country after country in the name of justice and peace.

And what followed Bush? A president who repudiated this ghastly legacy? No, Obama was a supporter of the same wars and continued them, even ramped them up. Did the left consider him a bad guy? Not really. With a handful of exceptions, his critics on the left were friendly critics. They were glad to put up with this because he was willing to do their bidding on the climate change front.

You think Democrat politicians don't exploit this? They surely do. In this sense, the climate issue is much like the pro-life cause on the right. If a politician pushes the correct buttons, it doesn't matter what else they say or do. They are no longer looked at with a critical eye.

The American left has long forgotten its roots. As Arthur Ekirch has explained, the left sold its soul to the state with the New Deal. Whereas it once opposed regimentation and industrial management of society, it turned to support exactly that. War was the next issue to go. The New Left in the 1960s held out the hope of capturing some of that early love of liberty on the left, even the anarchist impulse, but the New Left didn't last long. It was eventually swallowed up by machine politics.

The left today that supports world government to stop climate change bears little resemblance to the left of 100 years ago, which favored civil liberties and social liberality and was willing to do anything to end war. Now it has diverted its energies to a preposterously unworkable scheme based on pseudo-science. This is a terrible tragedy.

The left still has much to contribute to American public life. It can oppose the police state and the militarization of society. It can favor human liberty in most every area of life, even if it hasn't made its peace with the free market. Most of all, it can oppose American imperialism. But before it recaptures the spirit of its youth, it has to get rid of the preposterous idea that it should support the total state to manage what every generation has always known is unmanageable.

Food regulation is another area dear to the heart of environmentalists. In politics, even a little bit of familiarity breeds contempt. Here we see the state in all its loathsomeness: a class of pandering, mealy-mouthed, grasping special interests all fired up about what they will do with your money once they get or retain power.

Think about this. When people say government should do x, y, and z, they are really saying that these people should be given power to appoint other people to permanent positions of power to tell you and yours what they can and cannot do with their lives and property, and to take a rake-off for their trouble. That doesn't sound like a very good system, but to put the best spin on it we call it democracy, or simply: the modern state.

And so for the big issue today: should the modern state regulate what we eat? Must the state do so for our own health and safety? Do we owe our health and safety to government regulations or to the responsiveness of the well-capitalized market economy to our preferences and needs? You know my answers already, but consider that most people are all too willing to credit government for all that is good in the world, and equally prone to overlook market freedom as a source of all that we call civilizational progress. For example, they observe the coincidence of available, safe, and delicious food with federal regulations and conclude that the regulations brought about these good things.

History doesn't support this claim. In every carefully studied case of business and consumer regulation from the late nineteenth century to the present, we find something very different. Typically a large market player will make some improvement in safety, working conditions, consumer product transparency, or what have you, as a means of gaining competitive advantage (all well and good) and then lobby the government to make this wonderful improvement universal across the industry by force. The pretense is the improvement of all of civilization; the reality is the imposition of high costs on competitors. The improvement was brought about by the market, with government only arriving later to claim credit. This is one reason large market players are the main influences within the agencies that regulate them.

Let's move from abstractions to particulars. I claimed in an article on food allergies that no government regulation on labeling is necessary. The free market will encourage producers to reveal the contents of their products insofar as the consuming public desires such information and producers are free to provide it. They will provide as much or little as consumers desire to know. Even extreme demands concerning ingredient disclosure, ones that serve only a small niche organized around religion or specialized health concerns, can be served better by markets than government. The reason is that food producers profit only from service to buyers, not from fraud, sickness, or trickery (and in so far as fraud is involved, it can be settled through private litigation). If particular producers are unresponsive, there are a host of institutions that provide accountability: stores, consumer groups, special websites, or whatever.

This claim has called down a fury of protest from people who believe that only government can ensure that producers do not lie, trick, cheat, steal, and even kill. The arguments are not so much knee-jerk or absurd as they are highly conventional, just the sort of thing you hear from the TV news or read in the papers. The underlying bias is in favor of government not because the writer loves coercion or trusts power but because there is something that genuinely worries people about the idea of letting the "anarchy" of the market process determine what is produced and how.

Mind you, it is not socialists who are making these arguments but people who believe that they seek the best of both worlds: the productive power of the private economy, nicely curbed and trimmed here and there by regulations that help shape the patterns of production and curb the excesses of greed. This is a position that Mises said was impossible to sustain because regulations generate more problems that seem to cry out for more government fixes: and thus the disastrous march forward of the state through market institutions.

Whenever the government tells companies that they must do something one way and one way only, they are making alternatives illegal. When the German government says that beer can only be manufactured in a certain way, it is excluding all other ways. That leaves no room for innovation, even if innovation would be rewarding to the consumer. In France, for example, wine production must follow a prescribed method, and, as a result, the French wine industry is being destroyed as consumers choose wines from places that permit a free market in wine.

The US has fewer such regulations but we recently experienced the debunking of the government's preferred diet from mid-twentieth century until the present day, when the bureaucrats told us to eat maximum quantities of carbohydrates and not so much meat. Today, carb-avoiders and meat eaters are huge players in the market. Producers have responded to a very notable extent, and government only lately adjusted its recommended diet. (The very idea of a state-recommended diet strikes me as Soviet or something.)

By universalizing regulations on food, the government prohibits people from profiting by serving niche markets. Thank goodness the US doesn't prohibit agri-business and trade from improving their products by artificial means (fertilizers and the like), even as a vast market is available for organically grown foods.

Perhaps there's no accounting for taste, but business is always ready to serve the widest possible variety, provided government isn't there with its standardization and regimentation. If regulators say that the chaff must always be separated from wheat, it denies chaff eaters the opportunity to buy what they want and prohibits producers from meeting consumer demand.

A correspondent brought up the case of an Indian woman who was shocked that Americans do not have to sift rice to remove gravel, as she did in her native country. The writer said this is because in the US, the government does not allow rice makers to leave gravel in the rice. For this, he says, we should be grateful and say a prayer of thanks to left-liberal statism.

Now, I do not know whether or not there really is a regulation that tells rice makers that they must put no gravel in their rice. But I would hope there is not. In the first place, rice makers have a strong incentive to remove particles on which people might break their teeth. Put two rice bags on a grocery shelf, one that says sifted and the other that says unsifted, and we'll see which one sells. If no one sells sifted rice, there is an entrepreneurial opportunity for someone. This much we can know: no government bureaucrat has ever conceived of and implemented a viable, life-improving change that an entrepreneur hadn't thought of first.

What constitutes a life-improving change, we cannot always know in advance: I can easily imagine some rice snobs insisting that the sifting process ruins the flavor. Ultimately we must leave it up to the negotiation of consumer and producer to discover what should or should not be included or disclosed in food. The market mechanism is highly responsive to consumers' demands for taste and quality — and in fact this is another reason why people criticize the market. People say that it is a social waste to cater to every niche, every whim, every idiosyncrasy. As always, the free market gets blamed no matter what the outcome.

What's really at issue is a matter of history, causality, and faith. Do we owe our high standard of living to the market or the state? That is the question. The interventionists and statists credit the state because they get their causal connections mixed up (and this is because they have not studied economics) and they take a leap of faith to credit the government for things it cannot possibly do.

The state from the ancient world to the present has created nothing. It has only taken. The market, on the other hand, delivers more miracles every day than we can count. This isn't dogma; the evidence is so overwhelming that it takes a leap of faith to believe otherwise.

The next time you consider believing that the state can do anything better than the market, imagine a sea of permanent bureaucrats, lobbyists, pandering politicians, and those mad attendees at political conventions, and ask yourself: what can these people do that individuals in society — acting in their own self-interest, coordinating exchange through the market process, constantly testing decisions against economic feasibility and consumer demand — cannot do. The answer is nothing. There is nothing the state can do and that should be done that the market cannot do better.

Before you write to tell me that without the state, there would be a fly in every soup, please read Murray Rothbard's *Man, Economy, and State*. It is the best explanation of how society manages itself just fine without a band of respectable-looking criminals telling everyone what to do.

CHAPTER 5

Economic Egalitarianism: No One Deserves to be Better Than Anyone Else

A SHARP MARTIAN VISITING EARTH would make two observations about the United States — one true, the other only superficially so. On the basis of its ceaseless exercises in self-congratulation, the US appears to him to be a place where free thought is encouraged, and in which man makes war against all the fetters on his mind that reactionary forces had once placed there. That is the superficial truth.

The real truth, which our Martian would discover after watching how Americans actually behave, is that the range of opinions that citizens may entertain is rather more narrow than it at first appears. There are, he will soon discover, certain ideas and positions all Americans are supposed to believe in and salute. Near the top of the list is equality, an idea for which we are never given a precise definition, but to which everyone is expected to genuflect.

A libertarian is perfectly at peace with the universal phenomenon of human difference. He does not wish it away, he does not shake his fist at it, he does not pretend not to notice it. It affords him another opportunity to marvel at a miracle of the market: its ability to incorporate just about anyone into the division of labor.

Indeed the division of labor is based on human difference. Each of us finds that niche that suits our natural talents best, and by specializing in that particular thing we can most effectively serve our fellow man. Our fellow man, likewise, specializes in what he is best suited for, and we in turn benefit from the fruits of his specialized knowledge and skill.

And according to Ricardo's law of comparative advantage, which Mises generalized into his law of association, even if one person is better than another at absolutely everything, the less able person can still flourish in a free market. For instance, even if the greatest, most successful entrepreneur you can think of is a better office cleaner than anyone else in town, and is likewise a better secretary than all the other secretaries in town, it would make no sense for him to clean his own office or type all of his own correspondence. His time is so much better spent in the market niche in which he excels that it would be preposterous for him to waste his time on these things. In fact, anyone looking to hire him as an office cleaner would have to pay him millions of dollars to compensate for drawing him away from the extremely remunerative work he would otherwise be doing. So even an average office cleaner is vastly more competitive in the office cleaning market than our fictional entrepreneur, since the average office cleaner can charge, say, $15 per hour instead of the $15,000 our entrepreneur, mindful of opportunity cost, would have to charge.

So there is a place for everyone in the market economy. And what's more, since the market economy rewards those who are able to produce goods at affordable prices for a mass market, it is precisely the average person to whom captains of industry are all but forced to cater. This is an arrangement to celebrate, not deplore.

This is not how the egalitarians see it, of course, and here I turn to the work of that great anti-egalitarian, Murray N. Rothbard. Murray dealt with the subject of equality in part in his great essay "Freedom, Inequality, Primitivism, and the Division of Labor," but really took it head on in *Egalitarianism as a Revolt Against Nature*, which serves as the title chapter of his wonderful book. It is from Murray that my own comments here take their inspiration.

The current devotion to equality is not of ancient provenance, as Murray pointed out:

> The current veneration of equality is, indeed, a very recent notion in the history of human thought. Among philosophers or prominent thinkers the idea scarcely existed before the mid-eighteenth century; if mentioned, it was only as the object of horror or ridicule. The profoundly anti-human and violently coercive nature of egalitarianism was made clear in the influential classical myth of Procrustes, who "forced passing travellers to lie down on a bed, and if they were too long for the bed he lopped off those parts of their bodies which protruded, while racking out the legs of the ones who were too short."

What are we to understand by the word *equality*? The answer is, we don't really know. Its proponents make precious little effort to disclose to us precisely what they have in mind. All we know is that we'd better believe it.

It is precisely this lack of clarity that makes the idea of equality so advantageous for the state. No one is entirely sure what the principle of equality commits him to. And keeping up with its ever-changing demands is more difficult still. What were two obviously different things yesterday can become precisely equal today, and you'd better believe they are equal if you don't want your reputation destroyed and your career ruined.

This was the heart of the celebrated dispute between the neoconservative Harry Jaffa and the paleoconservative M.E. Bradford, carried out in the pages of *Modern Age* in the 1970s. Equality is a concept that cannot and will not be kept restrained or nailed down. Bradford tried in vain to make Jaffa understand that Equality with a capital E was a recipe for permanent revolution.

Now, do egalitarians mean we are committed to the proposition that anyone is potentially an astrophysicist, as long as he is raised in the proper environment? Maybe, maybe not. Some of them certainly do believe such a thing, though. In 1930, the *Encyclopaedia of the Social Sciences* claimed that "at birth human infants, regardless of their heredity, are as equal as Fords." Ludwig von Mises, by contrast, held that "the fact that men are born unequal in regard to physical and mental capabilities cannot be argued away. Some surpass their fellow men in health and vigor, in brain and aptitudes, in energy and resolution and are therefore better fitted for the pursuit of earthly affairs than the rest of mankind." Did Mises commit a hate crime there, by the standards of the egalitarians? Again, we don't really know.

Then there's "equality of opportunity," but even this common conservative slogan is fraught with problems. The obvious retort is that in order to have true equality of opportunity, sweeping government intervention is necessary. For how can someone in a poor household with indifferent parents seriously be said to have "equality of opportunity" with the children of wealthy parents who are deeply engaged in their lives?

Then there is equality in a cultural sense, whereby everyone is expected to ratify everyone else's personal choices. The cultural egalitarians don't really mean that, of course: none of them demand that people who dislike Christians sit down and learn Scholastic theology in order to understand them better. And here we discover something important about the whole egalitarian program: it's not really about equality. It's about some people exercising power over others.

At the University of Tennessee, the Office for Diversity and Inclusion explained that traditional English pronouns, being oppressive to people who do not identify with the gender they were "assigned at birth," ought to be replaced with something new. The diversity office recommends, as replacements for she, her, hers, and he, him, his, the following: ze [pronounced zhee], hir [here], hirs [heres]; ze [zhee], zir [zhere], zirs [zheres]; and xe [zhee], xem [zhem], xyr [zhere]. When approaching people for the first time, students were told, we should say something like, "Nice to meet you. What pronouns should I use?"

When the whole world burst out laughing at this proposal, the university was at pains to assure everyone that these were just suggestions. Of course, what are not suggestions are the thoughts all right-thinking people are expected to have about moral questions that have been decided for us by our media and political classes.

Another aspect of equality is, of course, income inequality. We are told how terrible it is that some people should have so much more than others, but rarely if ever are we told how much (if any) extra wealth the egalitarian society would allow the better-off to have, or the non-arbitrary basis on which such a judgment could be rendered.

John Rawls was possibly the most influential political philosopher of the twentieth century, and he advanced a famous defense of egalitarianism in his book *A Theory of Justice* that attempted to answer this question (among others). If I may summarize his argument in brief, he claimed that we would choose an egalitarian society if, as we contemplated the rules of society we'd want to live under, we had no idea what our own position in that society would be. If we didn't know if we would be male or female, rich or poor, or talented or untalented, we would hedge our bets by advocating a society in which everyone was as equal as possible. That way, should we be unlucky and enter the world without talents, or a member of a despised minority, or saddled with any other disability, we could still be assured that of a comfortable if not luxurious existence.

Rawls was willing to allow some degree of inequality, but only if its effect was to help the poor. In other words, doctors could be allowed to earn more money than other people if that financial incentive made them more likely to become doctors in the first place. If incomes were equalized, people would be less likely to go to the trouble of becoming doctors, and the poor would be deprived of medical care. So inequality could be allowed, but only on egalitarian grounds, not because people have the right to acquire and enjoy property without fear of expropriation.

Since no one in his right mind accepts full-blown egalitarianism, Rawls was bound to run into trouble. That trouble came in the form of his attempts to deal with equality between countries. Even the most dedicated egalitarian living in the First World doesn't seriously favor an equalization of wealth between countries. College professors who teach the moral superiority of egalitarianism during the day want their wine and cheese parties at night.

So Rawls came up with a strained and unpersuasive argument that although inequality between persons was outrageous and could be justified only on the basis of whether it helped the poorest, inequality between countries was quite all right. He then proceeded to give reasons that inequality between countries was quite all right, even though these were the exact reasons he had said inequality between individuals was unacceptable.

Even if egalitarianism could be defended philosophically, there is the small matter of implementing it in the real world. Just one reason the egalitarian dream cannot be realized involves what Robert Nozick called the Wilt Chamberlain problem; James Otteson has called something like it the "day two problem." In Chamberlain's heyday, everyone enjoyed watching him play basketball. People gladly paid to watch him play. But suppose we begin with an equal distribution of wealth, and then everyone rushes out to watch Chamberlain play basketball. Many thousands of people willingly hand over a portion of their money to Chamberlain, who now becomes much wealthier than everyone else.

In other words, the pattern of wealth distribution is disturbed as soon as anyone engages in any exchange at all. Are we to cancel the results of all these exchanges and return everyone's money to the original owners? Is Chamberlain to be deprived of the money people freely chose to give him in exchange for the entertainment he provided?

But the reason the state holds up equality as a moral ideal is precisely that it is unattainable. We may forever strive for it, but we can never reach it. What ideology could be better, from the state's point of view? The state can portray itself as the indispensable agent of justice, while at the same time drawing ever more power and resources to itself — over education, employment, wealth redistribution, and practically any area of social life or the economy you can name — in the course of pursuing the unattainable egalitarian program. "Equality cannot be imagined outside of tyranny," said Montalembert. It was, he said, "nothing but the canonization of envy, [and it] was never anything but a mask which could not become reality without the abolition of all merit and virtue."

In the course of working toward equality, the state expands its power at the expense of other forms of human association, including the family itself. The family has always been the primary obstacle to the egalitarian program. The very fact that parents differ in their knowledge, skill levels, and devotion to their offspring means that children in no two households can ever be raised "equally."

> Robert Nisbet, the Columbia University sociologist, openly wondered if Rawls would be honest enough to admit that his system,

if followed to its logical conclusion, had to lead to the abolition of the family. "I have always found treatment of the family to be an excellent indicator of the degree of zeal and authoritarianism, overt or latent, in a moral philosopher or political theorist," Nisbet said. He identified two traditions of thought in Western history. One he traced from Plato to Rousseau, that identified the family as a wicked barrier to the realization of true virtue and justice. The other, which viewed the family as a central ingredient in both liberty and order, he followed from Aristotle through Burke and Tocqueville.

Rawls himself appeared to admit that the logic of his argument tended in the direction of the Plato/Rousseau strain of thought, though he ultimately — and unpersuasively — drew back. Here are Rawls' own words:

It seems that when fair opportunity (as it has been defined) is satisfied, the family will lead to unequal chances between individuals. Is the family to be abolished then? Taken by itself and given a certain primacy, the idea of equal opportunity inclines in this direction. But within the context of the theory of justice as a whole there is much less urgency to take this course.

Nisbet took little comfort in Rawls's pathetic assurances. Can Rawls, he wondered,

long neglect the family, given its demonstrable relation to inequality? Rousseau was bold and consistent where Rawls is diffident. If the

> young are to be brought up in the bosom of
> equality, "early accustomed to regard their
> own individuality only in its relation to the
> body of the State, to be aware, so to speak,
> of their own existence merely as part of that
> of the State," then they must be saved from
> what Rousseau refers to as "the intelligence
> and prejudices of fathers."

The obsession with equality, in short, undermines every indicator of health we might look for in a civilization. It involves a madness so complete that although it flirts with the destruction of the family, it never stops to consider whether this conclusion might mean the whole line of thought may have been deranged to begin with. It leads to the destruction of standards — scholarly, cultural, and behavioral. It is based on assertion rather than evidence, and it attempts to gain ground not through rational argument but by intimidating opponents into silence. There is nothing honorable or admirable about any aspect of the egalitarian program.

Murray noted that pointing out the lunacy of egalitarianism was a good start, but not nearly enough. We need to show that the so-called struggle for equality is in fact all about state power, not helping the downtrodden. He wrote:

> To mount an effective response to the reigning egalitarianism of our age, therefore, it is necessary but scarcely sufficient to demonstrate the absurdity, the anti-scientific nature, the self-contradictory nature, of the egalitarian doctrine, as well as the disastrous consequences of the egalitarian program. All this is well and good. But it misses the essential

nature of, as well as the most effective rebuttal to, the egalitarian program: to expose it as a mask for the drive to power of the now ruling left-liberal intellectual and media elites. Since these elites are also the hitherto unchallenged opinion-molding class in society, their rule cannot be dislodged until the oppressed public, instinctively but inchoately opposed to these elites, are shown the true nature of the increasingly hated forces who are ruling over them. To use the phrases of the New Left of the late 1960s, the ruling elite must be "demystified," "delegitimated," and "desanctified." Nothing can advance their desanctification more than the public realization of the true nature of their egalitarian slogans.

The struggle for liberty must not be confused with egalitarian nostrums such as feminism. Might we gain the sympathy of the left by parroting their language of egalitarianism and loudly proclaiming our allegiance to the moral strictures of the state? It is not absolutely impossible, I suppose. But I consider it far more likely that the left will be amused at such transparent attempts at ingratiation, and go on viewing libertarians with the same contempt as before.

Of course, it's wonderful to collaborate on important issues with people who have different perspectives from ours. I should not be understood as opposing that. You would be hard pressed to find a more eclectic libertarian website than LRC. Mr. Libertarian himself, Murray N. Rothbard, was happy to talk with and learn from anyone he could, as his wide-ranging library, owned by the Mises Institute, amply attests.

But if we expect to trick people into becoming libertarians, we will fail. And if we think libertarian flirtation with egalitarianism is a good idea, we have already failed.

Yes, we do believe in unfashionable things like the abolition of anti-discrimination law. If we didn't, we would not be libertarians. Bound up in the principle of freedom of association is every defining libertarian principle: self-ownership, the meaning of property titles, and nonaggression.

It's easy to defend the rights of people who are popular and whose views are in fashion. It is much more difficult — thankless, even — to defend the rights of those whom society despises. Libertarians need not endorse or actually *be* such people — I know of no one proposing such a thing — but if we do not defend their rights we are frauds.

Some of what we believe may be hard for people to accept when they first hear it. But in the long run, they are more likely to be persuaded by a consistent and principled libertarian than by one who is obviously trying to curry favor with them.

Consider the example of Ron Paul. He gave straightforward libertarian answers to whatever questions he was asked during his presidential campaigns. As we all should, he got a sense of his audience and explained those ideas in ways they were most likely to understand and appreciate. But he never backed down. Was he opposed to anti-discrimination law? Yes. Did he dissent from the received version of the Civil War, from which the regime derives much of its legitimacy? Yes.

And so on down the line of unfashionable answers to the thought-controllers' questions.

The result? The single greatest increase in youth interest in libertarianism in its entire history.

Ron always conducts himself as a gentleman, of course, and his kindly demeanor, coupled with his pure and unrehearsed remarks, certainly added to his appeal. But people were drawn to him because unlike his focus-grouped opponents, he told them the truth, and without shame or apology.

Libertarianism is concerned with the use of violence in society. That is all. It is not anything else. It is not feminism. It is not egalitarianism (except in a functional sense: everyone equally lacks the authority to aggress against anyone else). It has nothing to say about aesthetics. It has nothing to say about religion or race or nationality or sexual orientation. It has nothing to do with left-wing campaigns against "white privilege," unless that privilege is state-supplied.

Let me repeat: the only "privilege" that matters to a libertarian *qua* libertarian is the kind that comes from the barrel of the state's gun. Disagree with this statement if you like, but in that case you will have to substitute some word other than libertarian to describe your philosophy.

Libertarians are of course free to concern themselves with issues like feminism and egalitarianism. But their interest in those issues has nothing to do with, and is not required by or a necessary feature of, their libertarianism. Accordingly, they may not impose these preferences on other libertarians, or portray themselves as fuller, more consistent, or more complete libertarians. We have seen enough of our words twisted and appropriated by others. We do not mean to let them have *libertarian*.

As Rothbard put it:

> There are libertarians who are indeed hedonists and devotees of alternative lifestyles, and that there are also libertarians who are firm adherents of "bourgeois" conventional or religious morality. There are libertarian libertines and there are libertarians who cleave firmly to the disciplines of natural or religious law. There are other libertarians who have no moral theory at all apart from the imperative of non-violation of rights. That is because libertarianism per se has no general or personal moral theory.

> Libertarianism does not offer a way of life; it offers liberty, so that each person is free to adopt and act upon his own values and moral principles. Libertarians agree with Lord Acton that "liberty is the highest political end" — not necessarily the highest end on everyone's personal scale of values.

> Libertarians are unsuited to the thought-control business. It's difficult enough trying to persuade people to adopt views dramatically opposed to what they have been taught throughout their lives. If we can persuade them of the nonaggression principle, we should be delighted. There is no need to complicate things by arbitrarily imposing a slate of regime-approved opinions on top of the core teaching of our philosophy.

Libertarianism is a beautiful and elegant edifice of thought and practice. It begins with and logically builds upon the principle of self-ownership. In the society it calls for, no one may initiate physical force against anyone else. What this says about the libertarian's view of moral enormities ranging from slavery to war should be obvious, but the libertarian commitment to freedom extends well beyond the clear and obvious scourges of mankind.

Our position is not merely that the state is a moral evil, but that human liberty is a tremendous moral good. Human beings ought to interact with each other on the basis of reason — their distinguishing characteristic — rather than with hangmen and guns. And when they do so, the results, by a welcome happenstance, are rising living standards, an explosion in creativity and technological advance, and peace. Even in the world's partially capitalist societies, hundreds of millions if not billions of people have been liberated from the miserable, soul-crushing conditions of hand-to-mouth existence in exchange for far more meaningful and fulfilling lives.

Libertarianism, in other words, in its pure and undiluted form, is intellectually rigorous, morally consistent, and altogether exciting and thrilling. It need not and should not be fused with any extraneous ideology. This can lead only to confusion, and to watering down the central moral claims, and the over-all appeal, of the message of liberty.

CHAPTER 6

Left Libertarianism

MARXISTS WERE NOTORIOUS FOR INFIGHTING over the most trivial differences. One group would secede from another, reverse the word order of the group it had seceded from, and declare itself the new and pure group. The first group, the new group would declare to the world, was part of the fascist conspiracy to suppress the coming workers' triumph, even though the differences between the two groups were completely undetectable even to an expert.

An informal debate taking place among libertarians these days, regarding whether people ought to be "thick" or "thin" libertarians, is of a different character. It strikes at the very heart of what libertarianism is.

The "thin" libertarian believes in the nonaggression principle, that one may not initiate physical force against anyone else. The thin libertarian thinks of himself simply as a libertarian, without labels. Most "thick" libertarians likewise believe in the nonaggression principle, but they believe that for the struggle for liberty to be coherent, libertarians must be committed to a slate of other views as well.

Before I proceed, let me anticipate an objection. Shouldn't I spend my time attacking the state instead of criticizing other libertarians?

Over the years at LRC we have left no stone unturned in exposing the evils and lies of the state, and building up the libertarian alternative. As a matter of fact, I have a book that continues in that tradition: *Against the State: An Anarcho-Capitalist Manifesto*.

Secondly, there's nothing wrong with what some people disparage as "infighting." A respectful exchange of ideas is how a school of thought develops. And I agree with Tom Woods: it is not true, as many allege, that libertarians are uniquely prone to arguments among themselves. Just observe the Democrats, the Republicans, your homeowners' association, Catholics, Protestants, Muslims — or, for that matter, just about anyone.

Proponents of a "thick" libertarianism suggest that libertarians are bound to defend something more than the nonaggression principle, and that libertarianism involves commitments beyond just this. One such proponent recently said, "I continue to have trouble believing that the libertarian philosophy is concerned only with the proper and improper uses of force." But no matter how difficult it may be for that person to believe, that is precisely what libertarianism is, and that is all it is.

We have been told by some libertarians that yes, yes, libertarianism is about nonaggression and private property and all that, but that it is really part of a larger project opposed to all forms of oppression, whether state-imposed or not. This has two implications for the thick libertarian. First, opposing the state is not enough; a real libertarian must oppose various other forms of oppression, even though none of them involve physical aggression. Second, libertarianism should be supported because the reduction or abolition of the state will yield the other kinds of outcomes many thick libertarians support: smaller firms, more worker cooperatives, more economic equality, etc.

Let's evaluate these implications one at a time.

To claim that it is not enough for the libertarian to oppose aggression is to fall into the trap that destroyed classical liberalism the first time, and transformed it into modern liberalism. How, after all, did the classical liberalism of the eighteenth and nineteenth centuries become the state-obsessed liberalism of the twentieth and twenty-first centuries? How did the once-venerable word *liberalism* become perverted in the first place? Precisely because of thickism. Sure, twentieth-century liberals said, we favor liberty, but since mere negative liberty — that is, restrictions on the state — doesn't appear to yield a sufficiently egalitarian result, we need more than that. In addition to restrictions on some state activity, we need the *expansion* of other forms of state activity.

After all, the new liberals said, state oppression isn't the only form of oppression in the world. There's poverty, which limits people's ability to make life choices. There's private property, whose restrictions limit people's ability to express themselves. There's discrimination, which limits people's opportunities. There's name-calling, which makes people feel bad. To focus entirely on the state is to miss these very real forms of harm, the new liberals said.

Sound familiar? Is this not precisely what many thick libertarians are now saying? Attacking the state is not enough, we hear. We must attack "patriarchy," hierarchy, inequality, and so on. Thick libertarians may disagree among themselves as to what additional commitments libertarianism entails, but they are all agreed that libertarianism cannot simply be dedicated to eradicating the initiation of physical force.

If some libertarians wish to hope for or work toward a society that conforms to their ideological preferences, they are of course free to do so. But it is wrong for them — especially given their insistence on a big tent within libertarianism — to impose on other libertarians whatever idiosyncratic spin they happen to have placed on our venerable tradition, to imply that people who do not share these other ideologies can't be real libertarians, or to suggest that it would be "highly unlikely" that anyone who fails to hold them could really be a libertarian. That these are the same people who complain about "intolerance" is only the most glaring of the ironies.

Thus the danger of thick libertarianism is not simply that vast chunks of the American population will fail to pass its entrance requirements, not keeping up every ten minutes with what MSNBC informs us is acceptable to believe and say. The danger is that thick libertarianism will import its other concerns, which by their own admission do not involve the initiation of physical force, into libertarianism itself, thereby transforming it into something quite different from the straightforward and elegant moral and social system we have been defending for generations.

Now for the second implication, that opposition to the state should be favored because it will yield egalitarian outcomes. (Of course, the abolition of the state will necessarily increase the level of egalitarianism from the point of view of *status*; the inequality of status between state officials on the one hand, who today may carry out all kinds of moral outrages with the legitimacy of the state to support them, and ordinary people, who are constrained by the traditional moral rules against theft and aggression, on the other, will no longer exist when the state disappears.) But what if it doesn't? The claim that firms will tend to be smaller on the free market, and that government policy encourages bigness in business, is far too sweeping a statement about far too complex a phenomenon. What if the absence of the state leads to no change in firm size, or in the employer-employee relationship, or in wealth inequality?

At that point, the question would become: to which principle are thick libertarians more committed, nonaggression or egalitarianism? What if they had to choose?

Likewise, the hatred of some classical liberals for the Church motivated them to confiscate Church property and impose restrictions of various kinds on Church activity. When it came down to a choice between their belief in liberty and their personal hatred for the Church, their personal hatred won the day, and their supposedly principled opposition to violence was temporarily suspended.

How people arrive at libertarianism is also immaterial. There are various schools of thought that culminate in the principle of nonaggression. Once there, we may of course debate what precisely constitutes aggression in particular cases, and other foundational questions within the general framework of the impermissibility of aggression. But if the school of thought you belong to takes you only partly toward nonaggression, it is not the case that you have discovered a new or better form of libertarianism. Such a case would mean only that you are partly a libertarian, not a different kind of libertarian.

Whether it's the claim that self-defense laws are "racist," that Bitcoin is "racist," or that libertarians ought to throw off "white privilege" — all of which have been advanced by libertarians claiming to have moved beyond our alleged fixation with the nonaggression principle — the various forms of thick libertarianism are confusing the core teaching of what we believe. None of these concerns have the slightest bit to do with libertarianism.

All of these additional claims are a distraction from the central principle: if you oppose the initiation of physical force, you are a libertarian. Period. Now how hard was that?

Conclusion

AFTER READING THIS BOOK, a question might come to your mind. We criticized "thick" pseudo-libertarians for trying to force egalitarian clichés onto libertarianism. Libertarians, we argued, are committed to people's property rights. So long as they respect the rights of others, people are free to do as they wish.

"If you say this, though," an objector might say, "aren't you guilty of the same fault from the other side? You denounce those who poison libertarianism with leftist ideology, but aren't you saying that libertarianism is right wing?"

This objection misses the point of the book. We are not trying to add to libertarianism. Precisely the opposite is the case. We are defending libertarianism as intended by Mises and Rothbard from those who want to undermine it. We do not think the State, or anyone else, should force people to accept anti-egalitarian values. Our contention is that, left alone, people will naturally be pro-family, devoted to Western culture, and unequal in all significant respects.

In sum, you don't have to accept conservative values to be a libertarian. But it helps.

Those who want to read more about these issues should consult our previous works, including *Against the State*. The books of Ludwig von Mises and Murray N. Rothbard are essential for understanding in depth what liberty is about. For the topics of this book, we recommend in particular two books: Mises, *Socialism*, and Rothbard, *Egalitarianism as a Revolt Against Nature and Other Essays*.

Index